Beautiful Lightning

Bogdan Octavian Sopterean

• Chicago •

Beautiful Lightning

Bogdan Octavian Sopterean

Published by
Joshua Tree Publishing
• Chicago •
JoshuaTreePublishing.com

13-Digit ISBN: 978-1-941049-69-3
Cover Image Credit: Vitaly Krivosheev

Disclaimer:

Printed in the United States of America

Dedication

To my sweet wife whom I adore with all my heart, to my beautiful daughter who fills my life with joy and happiness, and last but not least, to my "angel on earth," my dog who knew how to complete our circle of love once again.

Chapter 1

The extraordinary thing about someone's journey is its individual nature, and not one journey is identical to another. This true story is about a journey like no one else's, and I am very grateful to have been part of it.

In September 2005, I became part of someone's journey in a very special way when my wife and I decided to adopt a puppy. I have never had a pet before or had to be responsible for one, but I was getting more comfortable with the idea of having a dog because of my wife. She is the biggest animal lover I have ever known, and she has a humongous space in her heart for animals. If it were possible, she would have many animals of all kinds in our house.

Soon after we made the decision to adopt a puppy, we started to look around for where to start. So we mapped out the shelters in and around the north side of Chicago, which was where we lived at that time. But seeing that the number of shelters we found was much higher than we expected, we had to choose the first shelter we wanted to visit.

Of course, the closest location was the most convenient, but something inside of me pushed me to choose the shelter farthest from us. It was located on the south side of Chicago, and since we didn't have a work schedule that allowed us to visit that shelter during the week, we decided to wake up early on a Saturday morning to go.

There wasn't that much traffic on the road that day, but it still took us almost an hour to get there. After we parked the car, we got out; and as we were walking toward the front entrance, we saw someone playing with a dog in the yard on the side of the building. My wife and I stopped to watch them play for a few minutes—it seemed as if they were having a joyful time together. I grabbed my wife's hand eagerly and started to pull her toward the entrance.

As excited as I was at the thought of going home with a puppy, the closer we got to the entrance, the more nervous I became. But once I opened the front door and I could hear barking, I instantly became very curious to see the faces behind those barks.

We went inside, and a woman at the front desk greeted us and explained the adoption process. We didn't even need any directions to the area where the dogs were being held. We just had to follow the sound of the barking, and as soon as we entered the kennel, my heart began to slowly melt.

The kennel contained rows of cages with dogs that were different breeds and colors, all sizes and ages, hoping to be welcomed into a family; and not one cage was empty. Some dogs were barking loudly and wagging their tails, while others were just sitting in the corner of the cage, quietly watching people walk by. But the saddest thing to me was seeing some of the dogs just lying in their cages with their backs turned toward people as if they had given up.

Taking our time, we continued to look at the dogs. Then there she was—a small puppy with shiny black fur and pretty golden paws. She was resting quietly by the back wall of her cage, and she captured my attention. I took a look at the tag on the cage and learned her name, approximate age, and breed. Her name was Lola, and she was a pit bull mix that was approximately three months old.

"Hello, pretty puppy!" I said to her as I squatted down.

As soon as she heard my voice, she turned her head and came to me with her tail wagging enthusiastically. And the moment her beautiful honey-brown eyes stared into mine, I was already hypnotized.

I put my right palm on the front bars of the cage, and her front paws started reaching for my hand as if she wanted me to pick her up. She started licking my hand and then tried to push her small body through the cage door, hoping to get closer to me. She was already putting many smiles on my face, and the warm feeling from inside of my chest while I was petting her through the cold bars made me understand that she was the reason why that shelter was my very first choice.

As I continued playing and falling in love with her, I noticed a young guy that had stopped next to me and started staring at the puppy with what felt like wicked intentions. He took a quick look at her tag and, within about five seconds, grabbed it and quickly walked away.

The adoption process had been explained to us when we arrived, so I knew in order to start an adoption we needed to take the tag from the cage of the dog we wanted to adopt and bring it to the front desk. Remembering this, I immediately stood up and followed the guy because I wanted to find out the reason he grabbed the tag so hastily from the cage.

My wife followed me since she didn't have a clue why I just stood up and walked away, but as we followed the guy, I briefly explained to her what happened.

The guy went straight to the front desk. Everything happened so quickly that I thought maybe he worked there and he was going to make some changes on the tag. But I wasn't sure, so I waited next to the front desk, close enough to hear the conversation between him and the lady who worked there.

However, when I heard him say that he wanted to adopt the puppy I had already fallen in love with, I immediately got very emotional, and I wanted to shout out loud that it was not going to happen. Especially that I witnessed that he didn't even care to say hello or pet the puppy and only seemed interested in the information on the tag.

The more I watched him, the angrier I became, which made it really hard for me to be quiet and not say the thoughts that were spinning through my head. But I knew the smartest thing was to wait for him to go away so I could have a private conversation with the lady who handed him the application.

After she told him to fill out the application and bring it back when he was finished, the guy grabbed the paperwork and went to sit down in one of the chairs across the room. And as soon as I saw him sit down, I approached that same lady and told her that I would really love to adopt Lola too.

I was absolutely determined to convince her that the guy might try to take that puppy for the wrong reasons, and I wanted her to understand that it seemed he was only interested in her because she was a pit bull.

While I was giving her some of the details about what happened inside the kennel, I saw the guy out of the corner of my eye getting up and walking toward us, so I quickly changed the subject and asked the lady if I could get the adoption application forms. Unbelievably, as I was reaching for the forms, the guy just threw his paperwork on the desk in front of me and told the lady that he was finished filling it out.

It was bad enough that he seemed like he didn't really care about the puppy, but he also proved that he didn't have enough manners to wait until I finished talking with the lady. On the other hand, as we witnessed his behavior, I became less angry. I was just happy and grateful it was happening right there because it backed up my story about what happened inside the kennel.

The lady took his paperwork and told him that somebody would call and let him know their decision. But when he was asked if he would like to spend some time with the puppy before he left, I couldn't believe his response. He said that he would have plenty of time to do that when he comes back to pick her up. Then he just turned around and left.

I filled out the application to adopt Lola as well and returned it at the front desk to the same lady. On the other hand, instead of going home right away, we were happy to be able to spend some more time with the puppy outside of her cage, which could allow us to get to know each other a little bit better.

One of the shelter's volunteers brought her outside for us, and after twenty minutes of playtime, her lovable personality together with the many sweet kisses that we received from her made it very hard to leave her there. But before we had to say goodbye to her, I looked into her eyes, and with a kiss on her wet nose I said to her, "Don't worry. We'll be back for you."

On the way out, we thanked the lady from the front desk for her help, and we asked her to give us a call as soon as she would find anything out about the adoption.

By the time we got back into our car and looked at the time, we couldn't believe that we had already been gone from home for a few hours. And then we realized why we were both so suddenly so hungry. So as we drove back, we decided to stop to eat at an all-you-can-eat buffet close to home.

Luckily, there weren't many people inside, and we got seated right away. We ordered a drink, got a plate, and filled it with all different kinds of food from the buffet; but we hadn't eaten much before we realized our eyes were much bigger than our stomachs. Even so, we continued picking at our food and talking about Lola when all of a sudden my phone rang. I pulled it out of my pocket and answered, "Hello?" even though I didn't recognize the number.

"Mr. Sopterean?" asked a woman on the other end of the phone.

"Yes," I replied.

The woman told me that she was calling on behalf of the Chicago Animal Care and Control Shelter (CACCS), and she wanted to know if we were still interested in adopting the puppy named Lola. If so, she wanted us to let her know when we could come back to complete the paperwork so we could take the puppy home.

We quickly stopped picking at our food and got up so we could pay and leave. Then we were on our way to pick up a new member for our family.

Once we arrived back at the shelter, we immediately completed the adoption paperwork, and just as we finished, we spotted a volunteer in the hallway walking toward us with our puppy. As soon as the puppy saw us, her tail started to wag nonstop, and she began to pull more on the leash so she could get to us faster. I put the pen down on the table, and as I squatted down to pick her up, she started to lick my face. I took her in my arms, and I said to her, "I told you we'd be back for you."

Once we got to the car, I opened the door for my wife and placed our new puppy on her lap. I started the engine and looked at my wife with a huge smile on my face; and as soon as I leaned over to give her a kiss, our puppy happily started to lick our faces. I put the car in drive and said, "Let's go home."

We were very happy, and nothing could ruin our happiness that day—not even the heavy traffic we were caught in on the way home. As a matter of fact, the traffic jam gave us more time to play with the puppy and talk to each other about all the new names we were coming up with for her.

Because she had honey-brown eyes, a sweet personality, and shiny black fur accented with matching golden paws and eyebrows, we decided to change her name from Lola to Bella. That means beautiful in Italian, and beautiful she definitely was.

We were ready for the joy that Bella was going to add to our life but definitely not ready with what a new puppy needed. So we stopped at the PetSmart store near our home to purchase some of the necessary things.

The shelves were packed with many types of food and treats to choose from and with a vast variety of everything you would need or want for your pet. Plus, to be able to walk around with your dog inside the store was wonderful and extremely convenient. And then there wasn't a single dog there that wasn't wagging their tail enthusiastically, which made the store seemed like a piece of heaven on earth for all of them and the best place for us to shop.

We spent at least an hour walking around the store before we thought we had everything that we needed, but as we headed toward the checkout, we couldn't resist grabbing some extra toys that Bella was trying to pull off the shelf. So after we paid, we put everything in the trunk and drove home where we allowed Bella to sniff every inch of her new home.

It wasn't a large apartment, but it was big enough for the three of us. We had lived there for the past seven months, and because we had met some of our neighbors that had cats or small dogs, we assumed that having a puppy wouldn't create any problems with the landlord.

He was a man in his sixties with a strong personality and who always dressed very classy. He seemed like a very kind person, and because we never had a problem with him, we hoped that he wouldn't give us a hard time about getting a puppy. But after about a week, it was time to find out.

My wife and I were returning from our walk with Bella when we saw him doing some maintenance work outside the building. As we entered through the main gate of the building, we said hello to him and immediately introduced him to Bella. His reaction was genuinely nice about us having a puppy, but as we expected, he went straight to business. He requested copies of Bella's information and told us that the rent would have to be increased.

We didn't mind that. Bella was already bringing joy into our lives, and she was worth every extra dollar we would have to spend for rent. So we only needed to hear from him by mail about how much the rent would increase, and apparently everything else seemed all right. But things took a totally different turn when he decided to stop by in person and talk to us about the decision he made about us having Bella there.

He said he looked over the paperwork we gave him and decided that he didn't want to have a pit bull breed in his building. And his options for us were very simple. We would have to get rid of Bella, or we would have to move. It sounded unbelievable, but we didn't need much time to think over our options. We decided that we would move and began searching for a new place to live.

Sadly, the more phone calls we made, the more we realized that it was extremely difficult to find rentals that would allow us to move in with a pit bull mix. We just kept hearing the same thing over and over: "I am sorry, but I don't allow pit bulls in our apartment building" or "We are very sorry, but our association doesn't allow pit bulls."

While we were searching for another place to live, two of my childhood friends were trying to move from Pennsylvania to Illinois. They were looking for a temporary place to live in Chicago until they could find something for themselves, and they had no idea that we were trying to find also a new place to live with our dog when they called to ask if they could stay with us for a while. And I couldn't say no to them because they were like family to me. I was happy to be able to help them when they needed me, so less than a week later, we were all living in the same apartment together.

Bella was definitely the happiest out of all of us living together in that apartment because the more people she had around her, the more fun it was for her. Plus, we were all competing to gain her attention, with the goal of being her favorite, and she definitely enjoyed every second of it. As far as the landlord was concerned, if he would have asked why we suddenly had more people in the apartment, I was ready to tell him that I have my cousins visiting me for few days and nothing else.

Our efforts continuing looking for another place to live seemed worthless, so we even started asking everyone we met and everyone we knew to let us know if they came across any rentals without pet restrictions. And luckily for us, one of my wife's friends shared our story with her mom, and our problem touched her heart. She happened to own a two-floor apartment building and didn't care what breed our puppy was, how much she weighed, or about the gender. She had two dogs of her own, and she was just happy to be able to help us out.

She offered us the second-floor apartment, and the day we moved in was Saturday, October 1, 2005, the exact same day as my birthday. And for all the boxes we had to move, I couldn't say that I didn't have plenty of gifts to open on my birthday.

The apartment had three bedrooms, one bathroom, a large kitchen with a dining room next to it, and a spacious living room. We were positively expecting to pay a lot more for rent, but she even charged us the same price we were paying on the one-bedroom apartment that we had moved out of in Chicago. She knew the reason why we had to move out from there, and she didn't feel right to charge us more than we used to pay.

The new apartment was definitely more than enough for us but excellent for when we played hide-and-seek with Bella. It had plenty of closets for us to hide in, and I still can't forget the whiny cry Bella would normally make when it took her too long to find us. But she never gave up until her detective nose sniffed us out of our hiding spot, and then the second she found us we would see the biggest smile on her face—she loved that game as much as we did.

By the time we settled in the new apartment, the snow had already started falling, and watching Bella for the very first time in it, we had a feeling that winter would definitely be one of her favorite seasons.

As soon as her paws touched the snow and her nose dug deep into it, her excitement became uncontrollable. She began barking, running, and jumping all around us without slowing down or taking a break, and her facial expression playing catch with snowballs was beyond description, especially when she missed and the snowball would just vanish in the snow. She would always stare at me with such a confused look in her eyes, as if she wanted to ask me, "How did you do it?"

Her reaction made me feel like a magician, and that's a big reason why playing catch with snowballs also became one of my favorite winter games to play with her.

Slowly winter faded, and spring was back in no time, ready to cover the earth again with its mixture of many beautiful colors. It brought much warmer temperatures, which allowed people to enjoy spending more time outside with their dogs, and as the days became hotter, the beach along Lake Michigan was the perfect place for us to go as a family to cool off. It offered endless entertainment for us.

Bella had lots of fun romping in the sand, frolicking in the water, and catching the Frisbee from the air. But her favorite summer game was when my wife, Natali, would throw the ball and then Bella and I would race to see who got it first.

I always took off faster than her, but after five or six steps, Bella would pass me as if I weren't even moving. She'd be kicking sand back at me with her hind legs, with her neck stretched out, tongue flapping from her mouth, legs pumping like crazy, and all of her attention was focused toward where the ball landed. Then when she would pick it up and you could see the expression of sheer delight on her doggie face, it was hard not to smile at her happy exuberance and do it again even though I knew that it was impossible to get to the ball first.

And since the beach was only a few blocks away from our apartment, we tried to go there as many times as we could.

Chapter 2

Everything seemed to be going well in our lives, but unexpectedly, I received some bad news at work. The distribution company where I was working at that time had to downsize their number of employees because many of its nationwide stores were closing down. And since the employees with the lowest seniority were the first to go, I was part of the first wave of people to be laid off.

For a long time, I have admired the quote "When one door closes, another door opens, but we so often look so long and so regretfully upon the closed door that we do not see the ones open for us," so I tried not to let the layoff affect me much.

As soon as I got my unemployment, I immediately started searching online for another job. And soon after I began searching, I noticed an ad for the city of Chicago's police department. They were accepting new applications from people interested in becoming a police officer.

I had always been excited by and drawn to the drama of police work, and after I read about the process time and their requirements, I realized that I had everything they were asking for, so I decided to apply.

While trying to gather all the necessary paperwork for registration, my wife decided to apply with me too. I was extremely surprised by her decision because I knew she wasn't too excited about the danger that comes along with the job, but she loved the idea of trying to build a career together. She had always showed me her support and respect in everything I wanted to do or try, so I did the same thing for her.

And we soon realized that all the running and swimming that we did with Bella that summer at the beach was not only fun but beneficial for us. In thinking about it, Bella was probably the best running partner to train with because she never got tired and always had a smile on her face no matter what. As a result, we were one step ahead in preparing for the physical exam that we'd have to take during the hiring process.

I knew I shouldn't have any problems passing the physical exam, but I really started to get anxious when I realized I had to pass the written exam before even having a chance to take the physical exam. You see, I was born and raised in Romania, and I graduated from a physical education and sports university there. English is a second language for me, and knowing that there were a few thousand candidates trying to become police officers for the city of Chicago, motivated me to study harder than I used to when I was in college. So I brought home as many books from the library as I could that offered advice, information, and even some practice tests from various police departments across the country, and it definitely paid off.

On the other hand, Natali didn't need to prepare as hard as I did since she was born and raised and graduated college here in the United States. However, we both passed the written test and looked forward to taking the physical exam even though we didn't know when it would be. But thankfully, our lifestyle was keeping us both in shape, and we would be ready for it.

In the meantime, our Bella, with all the love and attention we offered her since we adopted her from the shelter, had become extremely attached to us. She could finally feel that she was part of the family and that our hearts would always beat underneath the same roof, but unfortunately for her as well as for us, she started to develop a separation anxiety.

Left home alone, she would try to destroy anything left on the floor, and her favorite snacks were always our shoes that weren't put in the closet. We were angry to find her with what was left of our shoes, but when we were showered with wet, sloppy kisses and joyous barks telling us how happy she was we came home, we quickly changed our mood.

Fortunately, since I was spending more time at home looking for a job while waiting on the hiring process for the Chicago Police Department, Bella's anxiety did not last much longer. That meant that we didn't have to keep her in a crate anymore while we were away from home, and that made us very happy.

A few months had passed since I got laid off, and finding a new job wasn't proving to be easy at all. I had no way of knowing how long the hiring process for Chicago Police Department would take, and the money from my savings account was diminishing quickly. So I decided that the best thing to do was to get my commercial driver's license, and that way, I could start working as soon as possible.

I learned everything I needed to know about semitrucks from a good friend of mine that I have known since my childhood that had his own semitruck. As soon as I had the permit that allowed me to drive while accompanied by a person who already had the commercial driver's license, my good friend took me with him to help me gain experience. He also allowed me a chance to get more comfortable driving a semitruck during a couple of his trips over the road.

The first trip was from Chicago to Baltimore and then from Chicago to Detroit. Both trips were during the winter, and of course, snow was not missing from the picture. It wasn't the ideal weather for learning how to drive an eighteen-wheeler, but by the middle of March, I was already driving on my own and finally making some money for my family. It was an over-the-road job, which meant a lot of driving hours away from home for five to six days at a time, but since it was the only available option at the time, I took it.

Knowing that I had to keep my physical condition for my next exam for the Chicago Police Department and I couldn't exercise the way I was accustomed to, I took with me a bunch of dumbbells and a jump rope and had to become familiar with regularly doing my workouts outside of my truck while parked at the truck stops.

Many people were staring at me, surprised or amazed while I was working out, but I did my best to ignore the people around me because I needed my exercise routine and the truck stops were the best places for a couple of reasons. There was plenty of space, and afterward, I could take a shower and have something to eat and then move on with my day.

It wasn't easy to be gone from home for days at the time, and the more months that passed by, the harder it was for me to leave home. Sometimes when I returned home after a long week, I didn't have any energy to do anything but stay home to relax, sleep, or simply enjoy being in my home.

I started to recognize that going over the road, driving to earn money, didn't feel like the right fit for me or my wife, so I began to search for local driving companies. Unfortunately, every job that I applied denied me because I didn't have enough driving experience, but I couldn't just give up. I continued to apply to different local driving companies, and my chance finally came at the beginning of July, when I was hired by one of the biggest soft-drink companies in the world.

The pay, the hours, and the benefits were good—I was extremely happy. My new hire orientation was right before the Fourth of July, and because that national holiday landed in the middle of the week, my start date would be at the end of the week.

Being together with my family and knowing that I had finally found a good local job made that Fourth of July holiday extra special. The spectacular parade and the many games that were available throughout the day for the community, along with the fireworks at the end of the day, kept us away from the apartment all day. By the time we finally returned home, it was almost midnight; and as soon as we hit the bed, we were fast asleep.

Suddenly I heard a sound that made me wake up for a second, but as I was ready to open my eyes, there was no more noise. I fell back to sleep but was quickly awakened when I heard the sound again. I realized the sound was coming from my phone. As I asked myself who would call me during the night and opened my eyes, I realized that it was already morning.

I picked up the phone, and it was my good friend who helped me get my commercial driving license. He knew that I just got the local driving job. Unfortunately, he got hit by some legal issues overnight that forced him to stay away from driving a commercial vehicle for about a year, and he had to ask me if I could help him by driving his truck for a while instead of starting work with the soft-drink company.

I wouldn't have any benefits driving his truck like I would if I worked for the soft-drink company, but since he was like family to me and the company he was working with at that time was a local driving company, I couldn't say no to him.

I started driving for him right away, and two months passed quickly when surprisingly, he learned from his lawyer that his problem was almost solved and that he would be able to drive again very soon. That was good news, and I was happy for him, but I also knew that would definitely put me back into search mode to look for another job given the fact that I certainly couldn't go back to the soft-drink company since I left them immediately after I got hired.

So without having other options and not knowing how long the Chicago Police Department process would take, I decided to speak with the owner of the company we were working with about the possibility of me continuing working with them even though I knew that I would have to purchase a semitruck on my own in order to work there. And two weeks later, I continued working for the same company, but that time as an independent owner operator.

Not too long after, we finally received the long-awaited letter from CPD with details about taking the physical exam, and we had about two months to get ourselves prepared. With my new job, there were many days that I left home around 3:00 a.m. and didn't return until after 7:00 p.m. Because I didn't always have time or the energy to get to the gym and keeping in shape was key to being ready for the physical exam, I decided to convert two of our bedrooms into exercise rooms. Besides, on my longer workdays, it would be more convenient to exercise at home than to go to the gym.

In one of the rooms, I had a bunch of dumbbells, a universal bench press, and a pull-up bar, while in the other room, I had a large punching bag and padded floor mats for stretching.

That was my intention anyway. However, oftentimes I would end up lying on the floor, napping, with Bella cuddling next to me. She always watched me work out from the doorway, and usually as soon as I was on the floor doing push-ups or stretching, she would come lick my face or want to cuddle. She didn't do it all the time, but I truly believed that she did it whenever she could feel that I needed to relax more than I needed to work out.

By the time the awaited CPD physical exam day came, we were definitely ready and enthusiastic but nervous at the same time. We both had butterflies in our stomachs, and trying to eat breakfast that morning was useless. So we felt it was best to just go and take the exam on an empty stomach.

At the time of our arrival at the testing location, the parking lot assigned for the candidates was almost full. Several people were trying to find any available spot to park, and we were one of them. A few good minutes later, we found a parking spot available, and after we parked the car, we started heading toward the end of the long line of people that were waiting alongside the building their turn to get inside. Thankfully, the line was moving fairly quickly.

As soon as we entered the building, we had to check in, where we got our group assignments for each of the different four physical exams. And then the fun began.

We had to run one and a half miles, do as many sit-ups as we could do in one minute, take the "sit and reach" flexibility test, and bench-press a percentage of our body weight. At the end of the day, we were given the results, and without surprise, both my wife and I passed without any problems.

We were extremely happy, but I was also very impatient to get to the next step of the hiring process because the time in between examinations felt for me like an eternity. If it were possible, I would have wanted to take all the exams in the same day so I could complete them all right away and start the police academy.

Besides, I was twenty-seven years old at that time, and I was ready to start a steady career that came with great opportunities to move up, a good salary, excellent health insurance, and a great pension. However, until then, all I could do was continue with my daily routine and look forward to the next letters from the CPD. But the day the letters finally arrived, we couldn't be more thrilled to open the envelopes, just knowing that we were one step closer to becoming Chicago police officers.

My wife opened her letter first, and as she started to read it out loud, she was congratulated for passing the physical exam, and then she was given the date and location for the next test, which was the psychological exam.

I was expecting to see the same information, but as I began to read my letter, I had to stop and stare at it in disbelief instead. My letter started out exactly the same as hers, congratulating me for passing the physical exam, but it continued with apologies that I couldn't advance further in their hiring process. And the worst part? There wasn't a single reason why!

I tried to analyze the situation that I found myself in, but since I had all their requirements to apply for the job and they accepted my application, plus I didn't fail any examinations, I couldn't come up with any good reason why they stopped my hiring process all of a sudden. So I decided to go along with my wife the day of her psychological exam, pretending everything was normal just to see what would happen.

And as we were waiting in line, inside the hallway of the college where the psychological exam was scheduled to take place, we noticed that a few candidates were turned away at the front of the line. Their facial expressions sure seemed very intriguing, which made it difficult for me and other candidates not to wonder what was going on. But we remained quiet while waiting our turn to check in and didn't ask a thing.

When we got closer to the front of the line, we saw two people sitting in the chairs behind a desk with a list of names in front of them. They were asking the candidates for their identification cards, and as soon as their name was found on the list, they were assigned to an exact classroom.

It was my turn to check in at the desk. My wife was right next to me, checking in with the other person from the desk. I was extremely nervous for what will happen next, but as soon as my name was found on the list, I thought that everything was all right and expected to be assigned to a classroom like everybody else. Unfortunately, I was asked to step aside and told that somebody would be with me shortly.

Meanwhile, my wife was assigned to one of the classrooms without any problems. She could hear everything I was being told, and she was as curious as I was about why I had to wait by the wall, but she had to go to the classroom she was assigned to. So after she wished me good luck, she left.

As I watched her walk down the hallway, I heard someone call my name. I turned around, and a man dressed in a police uniform holding a piece of paper straightforwardly asked if I had received a letter that informed me that I couldn't advance further in the hiring process.

I couldn't lie to him, but when I asked why I couldn't continue the hiring process, especially since I met all the requirements and passed the exams, I couldn't believe his answer. Very plainly, he said that their department has their own inside rules and he didn't have to give me any other answers other than the answers I had already received. Then I was asked to leave the building.

It all seemed like a bad dream that I was just waiting to wake up from, but the two and a half hours I waited for my wife to finish her exam definitely gave me the time to transition back into reality. And even if I was extremely disappointed with what happened to me, I still put a smile on my face for my wife to show her that I was very proud of her, which sadly made her jump immediately into my arms, thinking that everything was all right.

But as soon as she saw my eyes, she couldn't believe that my opportunity to become a member of the CPD was taken away from me that easily. And just like that, she decided that she no longer wanted to proceed with the hiring process. So when the officer in charge of her follow-up home interview called often and left plenty of voice mails, she never bothered to answer the call or return the message. And when she had been told that she had one month to gather all the necessary paperwork and set a date for the home interview and, if she didn't, she would be dropped from the hiring process, she also didn't do it.

However, the irritating part was that even after the month was over, she continued receiving phone calls from the same officer so they could set a date for a home interview, which was very infuriating for both of us since I was the one who truly wanted to be a cop.

I tried to stop thinking about it, but it seemed impossible without knowing the reason why they let me go. I even decided to try to find the answer by talking to a lawyer about the situation, and that just confused matters more. The lawyer convinced me that it was a discrimination act, and in order to find out, I would need to file a lawsuit. But no matter how unhappy I was with the CPD, the thought of suing them was the last thing on my mind.

Since I arrived in the United States from Romania at the age of twenty-two, I had to start from the ground floor with everything I did. Graduating college in Europe didn't really help much, neither did the fact that I didn't have any job history here. And that meant it made things more challenging to find work without experience.

I had to work as a prep cook, as a sous chef, as a busser, and as a waiter. I helped with installing HVAC units, learned how to lay tile on the floor or on the wall, tear down old walls, and build them back. No doubt it was hard, but I couldn't complain to anybody because it was a path I chose.

And as far as the lawsuit was concerned, I decided not to move forward with it. I have always believed that things happen for a reason, and I didn't feel the need to fight for that job. So I moved along with my life and continued to work as a truck driver.

The job was good, but since I was a child, I loved to work on projects that required a lot of imagination, and I wanted to find something that would just feel right for me. I wanted to find that special something that would bring me enjoyment, satisfaction, and a sense of accomplishment at the end of the day.

Chapter 3

Thankfully, by the end of the year, my police story seemed like it never happened, and as we started getting ready for Christmas season, I eventually stopped talking about it.

Soon we decided to start our holiday shopping, and of course, Bella was the easiest family member to shop for since we didn't have to overanalyze the gifts we bought for her. We could have given her the smallest toy ever and she would still be extremely excited. But we knew exactly what she loved, and that's what we got for her.

On the other hand, searching for gifts for each other was a little more challenging because we both took pleasure in showing appreciation for one another, and the extra time spent in finding or creating that extra special gift for each other was well worth it. However, that year I received my gift much earlier, and I couldn't have been more thrilled about it.

It was a few weeks before Christmas, and after a long, busy workweek, as I was trying to catch up on my sleep one Saturday morning, I was awakened by my wife with a sweet, gentle kiss on my cheek.

"Good morning, sleepy face. It's time to wake up," she said to me as she sat down on the bed next to me.

I tried to open my eyes, but I couldn't. They felt as if they were glued shut, and I wanted to sleep some more. But once she started to grip my hand and squeeze tightly, she made me open my eyes curiously.

She was staring at me with a huge, radiant smile with tears filling her eyes.

"I'm pregnant!" she exclaimed proudly.

When I heard that, I quickly jumped out of bed, took her into my arms, and started showering her with kisses. That was when I realized that she was holding a pregnancy test in her left hand. She handed it to me, and as soon as I saw the two lines on the test that indicated she was pregnant, I got more excited and couldn't stop kissing my wife.

Bella came into the room, running and wagging her tail excitedly. She didn't know what was going on, but she always came to us when she heard kisses, and she wanted to be part of celebration.

We couldn't be happier now that we knew we were going to be parents, but as eager as we were to share the news, we didn't want to tell anyone our big secret right away so we wouldn't jinx anything.

Unfortunately, Natali started to have severe morning sickness that usually lasted throughout the entire day, and it began to affect her in every way, including how she performed at work. She was a personal trainer, and it became increasingly difficult to train her clients at the gym when she needed to run to the bathroom frequently to throw up. So at that point, we decided the best thing for her was to take time off from her job and try to enjoy the pregnancy.

She began reading and learning as much as possible and not just about what to expect while she was expecting but also after the baby was born. That gave her peace of mind and a better understanding of what to expect when pregnant, and as we felt more secure about everything, we finally shared our big secret with family and friends.

I couldn't know how I would be as a dad, but I certainly found out more about myself as Natali began to show her pregnancy bump, especially when we were in a crowded space. I would always walk a step in front of her just to make sure nobody could bump into her belly. Maybe it was silly of me to do that, but I felt great about it. Besides, I wasn't the only one acted differently around Natali while she was pregnant.

Our sweet Bella became also much more suspicious and analytical of approaching strangers than she ever was before on their walks outside together. Natali enjoyed every second of it.

Once summer arrived, Natali's due date, as well as her birthday, was soon approaching, and we were extremely happy to have my parents offer to come and live with us for a few months to help us out.

They flew here from Romania at the end of July, knowing that Natali was due at the beginning of August, and we definitely couldn't make any plans for Natali's birthday since few days before her birthday we were still waiting for our baby born to reveal herself. We even started joking that our baby might want to be born right on Natali's birthday, as a gift. And wouldn't you know it, Natali went into labor on Saturday, August 15, 2009, around 1:00 a.m., exactly on her birthday.

At that time, I was in a very deep sleep in our bed when all of a sudden I could feel my body rocking back and forth. Natali's hand was on my shoulder, rocking me back and forth, and with a quiver in her voice exclaimed, "Babe! Babe! Wake up! I'm having contractions!"

I stood up right away and turned on the light. Her facial expression looked as if she was happy and scared at the same time. In the meantime, my parents woke up too because they heard us talking in our bedroom.

The contractions were happening more than ten minutes apart, and since the hospital was just a few blocks away from us, Natali decided to stay home until the contractions were closer together. But an hour passed and the contractions were still more than ten minutes apart. And since we were still awake, we started singing happy birthday to Natali, after which she lay down on bed to try to get some more sleep. Afterward, we all decided to close our eyes afterward, and by the time we woke up again, it was already 7:00 a.m.

Natali's contractions were still ten to twelve minutes apart, but that time, Natali wanted to go to the hospital for a checkup. So we got dressed and headed over there.

When we arrived at the hospital, everything was supposed to go according to a birth plan that Natali had written down and e-mailed to them months before her due date. It was an option that the hospital offered to every pregnant woman delivering a baby there, and Natali took advantage of it. She wanted to have our baby girl born as naturally as possible and with as few procedures or medications as possible.

Once we checked in, after a quick exam from the nurse, we were told that Natali was definitely in early labor. But since it could be a while before her contractions would get closer together, we were given the option to go back home and wait there. So that's what we did.

Natali took a warm bath, and then she stretched down on the couch in front of the TV in the living room with Bella by her feet. Ten minutes later, they were both asleep.

My parents and I were being as quiet as we could, but in spite of it, her contractions continued to wake her up on and off again. They became closer together, more painful, and they started to last longer. We thought that being home would make Natali more comfortable, but the stronger her contractions became, the more anxious she was getting. And about that time, she decided it was time to go back to the hospital and stay there.

So by two o'clock, we checked in again and were assigned a room that pretty much had anything that we needed. It had a private bathroom and a small pullout chair next to the bed Natali was in, which gave me the perfect view of both monitors she was connected to.

One monitored the sequence of Natali's contractions, including her pain level, and the other screen monitored the heartbeat of our unborn baby girl.

The more time passed, the stronger and more intolerable her contractions became. Watching her going through each contraction made me feel helpless, and the only thing that I was able to do was just paying attention to the contractions monitor, which gave me an advanced notice before she would feel the contractions. So that way I could begin to massage her lower back to try to ease her pain right away.

That day certainly didn't seem like a birthday to her but definitely sounded like one. Friends and family members were trying to get ahold of her to wish her a happy birthday, and since her cell phone was at home, everyone called my phone.

I couldn't answer everyone's phone calls every time. Few hours passed quickly; Natali was still in labor, and my phone continued to keep ring. Friends and family kept trying to get ahold of Natali, but that time it was our parents.

Since the hospital had a visitor restriction policy due to a virus that was spreading rapidly around the world, named H1N1 influenza, a.k.a. the swine flu, I was the only one allowed in the room, and our parents were getting worried not being able to know what was going on.

They expected me to keep them posted with the latest news as often as I could, but Natali wanted all my attention. At that point, everyone became stressed, including me, and trying to put everyone at ease wasn't easy at all. But I tried my best to share the latest news with them once in a while in between Natali's contractions, and luckily it worked.

Natali's birthday had come and gone. She still wanted a natural birth, but once our baby's heart dropped below eighty beats per minute, things were ready to take a different turn. Her contractions were still not getting closer together, and her cervix had only partially dilated, so she agreed to have her labor induced.

The contractions became closer and much stronger, but she was still barely dilated. And then a portable bathtub was brought into our room so she could try to relax and release some tension, but that only worked for a short time.

It had been a long time since Natali started labor. Her birthday was long gone, yet her water still hadn't broken. So that had to be done by the doctor also. It was then that we were told a C-section might be needed since things were not progressing according to plan.

We didn't want to risk anything, but as long as the baby was fine, my wife still wanted to try for a natural birth. However, a few more hours passed, and when the baby's heartbeat dropped below eighty beats per minute again, it was best to have the C-section.

The nurses started to prep Natali for surgery immediately, and I was very relieved to find out that I could be in the room with her during the surgery. So after I got changed into everything they gave me, which included a surgical shirt, pants, hat, mask, gown, boots, and gloves, I was escorted into the delivery room.

It was my first time inside of an operating room, and seeing all the surgical instruments ready to be used for the operation instantly raised my adrenaline to the roof. My wife was already given an epidural, and she was lying on the table, waiting for the doctors to begin performing the surgery.

I grabbed her hand and sat down on a chair next to her head. Below her chest was a curtain used as a divider between the doctors and us to make sure that we couldn't see them performing the surgery. All I could see was the doctors' and the nurses' heads and shoulders.

Once they started, all the blood on their gowns and gloves increasingly piqued my curiosity, and it just made me want to see more. And as soon as I'd try to sneak a peek over the curtain, Natali would squeeze my hand and pull me to sit back down next to her. She just didn't want me to look and see my reaction. In fact, she begged me not to. So I listened to her and sat back down, but all bets were off when I heard my baby girl cry for the very first time. It was already past midnight, and August 17 was her day to be born.

I immediately stood back up and watched over the curtain. One of the nurses was holding our baby in her hands and rushed to clean her off on the table that was next to us. As soon as Natali glanced at the baby, a small stream of tears began running down her cheeks. Quickly, I took out my digital camera and started taking a few pictures while the nurse was still cleaning off the baby.

My wife was waiting impatiently to hold the baby, and the nurse easily realized that. So she picked the baby up and laid her on Natali's chest for a moment where we could see our baby girl's eyes for the very first time. They were wide open and just staring right into my wife's eyes. Suddenly, her pink rosebud mouth opened, and she yawned, making my wife yawn as well. The exhaustion from the days and nights of labor was almost too much for both of them. The nurses took the baby to the nursery to clean her up some more while the doctors finished up with the rest of the surgery.

By the time they moved Natali back into her room, she was almost asleep. I was also exhausted, but before I lay down on the pull-out couch next to Natali's bed, I called our parents to let them know that everything was all right so they could also relax and get some good sleep. And then when I finally closed my eyes a bit, I heard a knock at the door, and the door opened. It was a nurse bringing our baby to our room in her bassinet.

Natali was still sleeping, but just as soon as the baby made her first sound in the room, Natali's eyes opened instantly. I stood up excitedly, wanting to pick up and hold our baby girl in my arms, but when I looked inside the bassinet and saw this tiny, fragile thing wrapped in a blanket, I hesitated to pick her up. I was scared that I would drop her or squeeze her too hard. The nurse looked at me, and she started to giggle.

"You're not the only man who is afraid to hold a newborn baby. Allow me to help," she said.

First, she showed me how to hold my arms, and then she picked the baby up from the bassinet and put her in my arms very gently. Natali was watching me with the proudest smile on her face, but my body was frozen in fear, thinking that I might drop her. So I slowly stepped toward my wife and gently handed our newborn baby girl to her.

Amazingly, our baby opened her mouth and instinctively latched onto the nipple and began suckling until she fell asleep. Natali gave me a big smile, and after I placed our baby back into her basinet, she quickly fell asleep too. And then as I sat back down on the pull-out couch, I passed out as well.

Natali's recovery time at the hospital lasted two days after the cesarean, so by Wednesday afternoon, we were released and on our way home with our new family member Sydney Jolie Sopterean.

Bella's capability to realize that something was different about us was noticeable. Normally, she was very excited to see us and would run to greet us. But that time, as soon as we entered the home, she was acting totally different.

She started to come toward us slowly and cautiously with her tail still and her ears pointing straight up, and her nose was inhaling and exhaling vigorously. However, it didn't take her much time to sniff all of us until her tail started to wag excitedly again.

As the days passed by, Bella seemed to get more and more attached to the baby, and she always wanted to be where Sydney was. It seemed as though she appointed herself as Sydney's guardian, protecting her like she was her own puppy, which she pretty much proved it from the very first party that we had at our home when we invited a bunch of friends and family to meet our new addition to the family and celebrate with us.

With all those people inside our home, Bella refused to leave Sydney's side the entire evening. When someone held Sydney in their arms, Bella was right away at their feet and just stare at them, but when she was in her crib, Bella would just lie down on the floor next to her and not move.

She certainly enjoyed being Sydney's guardian as much as she could, but as the time passed by, Sydney wasn't any longer just a baby and Bella had to change as well.

Sydney was almost three years old, and she loved to have tea parties for all of us, including Bella. She enjoyed playing dress-up with her, and best yet, Bella even patiently listened to the musical concerts Sydney conducted or performed throughout the house. And then sometimes she would even hold Bella's front paws and slow-dance with her.

Bella never seemed to mind any of those things, and that's the reason why Sydney couldn't see any longer Bella just as her dog but the best sister in the world who had always been with her on good or bad days. Like she was on this particular day, when Sydney would absolutely never forget.

Chapter 4

It was a typical hot summer day in Chicagoland until the weather started changing unexpectedly.

I was at work, driving, when I could hear the sound of thunder rumbling somewhere in the distance. It got so hot, the tar on the road began to melt. In the side mirrors of my truck, I saw that the sky was getting darker behind me and rolling in faster than I was driving. The thunderous rumblings in the distance grew steadily louder. With each passing mile, the sky became darker and darker until it was so dark that day had almost turned into night.

I was undaunted by the idea of enduring a full-blown thunderstorm while I was driving because it wasn't unusual for me, but since it looked like it was headed toward the area where we lived, I called my wife to warn her. She was already home from the gym with Sydney, and they were snuggling on the couch with Bella watching cartoons.

By the time I got off the phone, the wind began to blow, flashes of lightning were racing through the sky, and buckets of rain came pouring down, which forced me to slow down considerably. A few more miles down the road and the thunderstorm had erupted in full force. Windswept rain reduced the visibility to zero, and I had no choice but to pull off to the side of the road and wait patiently for the rain to stop.

As the thunderstorm began to move away as quickly as it appeared, I knew that it was just a matter of time until the storm would hit the area where we lived.

I wasn't too concerned about my girls because I knew they were home and safe, but knowing that both Sydney and Bella were very afraid of bad weather, my heart wanted to be with them to make them feel safe.

The lightning was still flashing in the distance throughout the dark sky, and then some strong booms of thunder could still be heard. It looked like the storm was not ready to give up. And just as I was going to call to check on them, my wife called.

"Babe, our building got struck by lightning!" she said to me.

I could hear the concern in her tone, but because of her calm demeanor, I couldn't believe she was telling the truth.

At first, I thought she was joking, but when she described what happened and I could hear my daughter in the background repeating, "Daddy, I'm scared!" I knew that it had to be real.

Besides staying on the phone and trying my best to calm down my daughter, I couldn't do much for them. And then when I finally got home, I couldn't believe what I saw.

Incredibly, the lightning strike cracked the left side of the window frame near the couch where the girls sat while watching cartoons. It completely opened it and even exposed a nail. Natali said that it started smoking so badly that she was worried it would start a fire. There were even spots on the blinds that were scorched. Plus, the TV and the DVD player were destroyed.

Natali described the lightning strike as the loudest fire cracker pop sound she had ever heard, and they both still had really loud ringing in their ears. All three of them were terrified, and I couldn't believe that our apartment was actually struck by lightning.

Somehow, I had to find a way to put my daughter at ease because she was still frightened by the whole thing, so I told her that as long as she was with Mommy, Daddy, or Bella during any bad weather, everything would be okay.

Sydney gave me a big hug and said, "Daddy! That was so loud. I am very scared of lightning!"

However, after that day if there was any bad weather, they definitely didn't want to be near any windows, and if we were home together, we'd try playing board games or reading books, given the fact that reading was one of Sydney's absolute favorite things to do.

Since she was little, she spent plenty of time at the library with my wife, and as a result, reading books with her was something that we started to do regularly. Each trip to the library would always end up in bringing home gigantic piles of books, and she would go through all of them as fast as most kids would go through a bowl of ice cream.

But when winter came and forced us to spend more time inside of our apartment, the piles of books were growing considerably that Sydney's room began to resemble a small library that I even started joking with her that the public library would probably have to close their children's department until they got their books back.

On the other hand, as much as she loved her books, she loved to play with Bella in the snow too. Once snow fell on the ground and accumulated enough to play in, Sydney right away would drop everything and ask us to go out and play in it.

We all as a family loved winter activities involving snow, and watching my daughter having that much fun made me want to introduce her to one of my personal favorite winter sports: snowboarding.

She was already three and a half years old, old enough to give it a try; so after we spent Christmas and New Year's Eve with our family, we went and bought snowboard equipment for her. My wife and I already had our own equipment. Then we decided that a short trip to Wisconsin on a Saturday would be enough to give my daughter a proper introduction to what snowboarding would feel like. And since we didn't want to spend the night there, two of my friends that we usually went snowboarding with decided to join us.

The resort was three hours away from where we lived, and knowing that we would need to leave very early to have plenty of time on the slopes, we left Bella at the PetSmart hotel the night before.

The temperature outside when we left was lower than we expected, and by the time we got there, the temperature dropped even more, forcing us to add one more layer of clothing on Sydney. But constantly going up and down the bunny hill with her kept us warm for the next few hours.

When my girls decided to take a break and go inside to eat and drink something warm, I met up with my friends on the advanced slopes, where we could chase each other and try different tricks and jumps; but as soon as Sydney and Natali were ready to come back out and practice some more, I was right back on the bunny hill.

I was expecting that the many falls my daughter took throughout the process of learning how to snowboard would take away from the enjoyment of sliding down the hill on a board, but I was totally wrong. She seemed to be enjoying snowboarding as much as us.

With all the fun we had, time was passing quicker than we expected, and I couldn't believe it was already 4:00 p.m. At that time, all the slopes and lifts shut down for an hour, which was the perfect time to get something to eat and warm up a bit also.

By the time we all finished eating, it was around 5:00 p.m., and because the outside temperature dropped again, Natali decided it was too cold for Sydney to go back out. So while they stayed inside by the fireplaces, I went back out with my friends. But before I went, Natali made me promise that I would be careful out there, and I promised her.

Once I was back on the slopes, I started taking a couple of small jumps, which made everything more fun, and continued trying to do some new small tricks and jumps that I didn't think would hurt me. Everything was going smooth that I felt comfortable enough to try some more challenging jumps. So I began to ride on one of the slopes that had on its last stretch two consecutive long jumps, and it ended with a vertical obstacle that had on top of it a very large horizontal wooden log.

Usually people slide up the obstacle, hit the log with the bottom of the snowboard, and slide back down. And that's exactly what I did in the beginning, but I wanted to do something different. So I decided to jump over the wooden log and land on the other side.

At first, I was kind of nervous. But after I did it once, I felt amazing, so I decided to do it again. And that time, I knew that with a little more speed, the jump over the wooden log would be much easier, and it definitely was.

In the meantime, the dropping temperature already changed the texture of the snow. It became icy. So I decided to go for one more round before I'd call it a day, but I should have stopped right there.

However, the props that I received from the other snowboarders and skiers who saw me jump over the log boosted my ego, and I decided to do it one more time before we went home. And that time, I decided to jump all three obstacles in the same run without stopping.

I hopped on the ski lift, and as I was on my way back up the mountain, a voice inside my head was trying to change my mind, but I didn't listen to it.

I hopped off the ski lift, and after I checked my bindings, I started going down the slope. I cleared the first jump with a smooth landing and continued toward the second jump. I nailed the landing on the second jump and kept going straight toward the last jump to gain more speed.

I started to slide up the obstacle, and with the extra speed I gained, I knew it shouldn't be a problem going over the wooden log—I did it before. And then I was just about over the log again when the back of my snowboard scraped the log and immediately caused me to lose my balance entirely.

I was approximately fifteen feet in the air and couldn't do much to regain my balance. I tried desperately like a fish out of water, but my body shifted the opposite way, and I slammed flat on the ground onto the right side of my body. Luckily, I had the instinct to stretch out my right arm underneath my head, just enough to take away the full impact of my head hitting the ground. That day, I wasn't wearing my helmet.

I instantly felt sharp pain going through my hips, and my right shoulder became numb. I froze in fear while my brain was thinking about my possible injuries. An intense pressure around my hip area escalated the pain I felt in my body, and because my feet were still attached to the snowboard, I felt the need to release them.

I was flat on my back when I asked one of my friends to untie them, but as soon as my feet were released, I felt the most excruciating pain in my entire life. My legs instantly collapsed outward, and every move I made brought another sharp pain to my hips. They wanted to bring the first-aid crew, but I told them not to because I wanted to wait a few minutes with the hope that I might feel better.

Five minutes or so had passed, and then I asked them to pick me up so I could find out if I would be able to stand on my own. They grabbed my arms and pulled me up, and as soon as they let go of me, I instantly collapsed onto my knees and fell flat on the ground. My legs were unable to hold my body weight.

I stubbornly continued to wait, hoping I would feel better, but after ten minutes of shivering while I lay on the frozen snow, I couldn't ignore the fact that my body was getting cold and the pain was escalating much faster. By then, I knew that I wouldn't feel better. In fact, I felt worse. So my friends brought the ski patrol to me, and after a couple of questions and a quick examination, they put me on a stretcher and took me to their medical area.

As soon as they got me inside of the medical building, they put me on a table and covered me with a warm blanket. I was expecting to get any available pain medicine, but unfortunately, they weren't allowed to give me anything since they didn't have all the information yet about my injuries. I was still shaking, and the excruciating pain started to fill my eyes with tears.

As I began to tell myself that everything would be okay, I saw Natali walk in, holding our daughter in her arms, and my friends came in the room soon after. Her face looked scared, concerned, and angry at the same time because earlier that day she made me promise to be careful and I didn't keep my promise.

She wanted to call the ambulance immediately when she saw me in pain, but because I didn't have health insurance at that time, going to the hospital was my last resort. I tried my best to bear the pain as much as I could, but after an hour passed, my pain level was rising by the minute, and I still couldn't move my legs without excruciating sharp pains throughout my hips. And then my lower back started to hurt, too, and the numbness in my right shoulder began to fade into throbbing pain. Sooner or later, I had to admit that I wasn't getting any better, so I agreed to call an ambulance that took me to the nearest hospital where I immediately received a full-body CAT scan, and I finally got something temporary for the pain.

As we were waiting for the results, my pain was coming back with a vengeance, and it was worse than ever before. My wife was getting ready to call the nurse when the doctor rushed into the room with the results of my body CAT scan. It showed that I might have some internal bleeding, and because they were a small hospital with limited capabilities, they needed to rush me immediately to a different hospital.

They quickly put me in the ambulance, where my wife stayed by my head while my friends had our daughter in the car following us from behind. It took us thirty long minutes to get to the second hospital, and once we arrived there, the paramedics were already waiting for us to take me directly into the ER. There, I was lifted onto a hard-narrow table where I was turned and rolled so my entire body could be scanned and X-rayed to discover the extent of my injuries.

Fortunately, the internal bleeding was ruled out, but at the same time, they discovered the reason for my excruciating pain. I had two fractures along my right pelvic ring, a fracture along my left pelvic ring, a fracture of my sacrum, and torn ligaments in my right shoulder. The size and the nature of the fractures on my pelvic rings instantly put me on the edge of needing surgery to stabilize them or letting them heal on their own, but I had to wait until the next morning to find out since the doctor wanted to get a second opinion from another surgeon before his final decision.

From that moment, my friends couldn't do anything else to help me, so they returned home while we had to remain at the hospital.

Lying on my back was the only position that was somewhat comfortable in bed in the hospital, and even though I was loaded up on painkillers, every move I tried to make was still causing excruciating sharp pains throughout my hips. It was impossible to get some good rest since once in a while I needed to rearrange somehow to try to find a comfortable position, and that kept me awake for the remainder of the night.

By that morning, we should already have been home; so when my parents called to see how Sydney's first time snowboarding experience was, I felt like I should withhold the entire truth from them and keep it as simple as possible. I told them, "Because Sydney had a lot of fun, we decided to stay an extra day," and nothing else.

I felt bad lying to them, but they couldn't possibly know what happened to me, and they couldn't have done anything since they were back in Romania—I just didn't want them to be worried. As I was trying to wrap up our conversation so my parents wouldn't get suspicious, the doctor came into the room, holding a bunch of papers in his hand. I immediately hung up the phone and focused all my attention on him.

After a long conversation with the other surgeon, they decided that I could go without surgery. However, I would still have to stay in the hospital until I was able to stand up from the bed and take a few steps with the crutches on my own. Those were the minimum requirements in order for me to be released from the hospital, and the rest depended on me.

Since it was a matter of time until I would be released, I insisted that Natali and Sydney go home. They were definitely better off home, plus we were supposed to pick up Bella from the PetSmart hotel that Sunday morning. But they didn't even want to hear me talking about them leaving me alone. They wanted to stay with me as long as I had to be there, so Natali called the PetSmart hotel, knowing that Bella was in good hands, and extended her stay until further notice without any problems. And then the last thing remained to do was to push myself to prove to the physical therapist that I was ready to go home.

The following day, I started to take baby steps in everything I was doing, but two days later, I felt ready enough to try to pass their minimum requirements.

It took me a while to get up from the bed because of my torn ligaments in my right shoulder, but I couldn't believe the exhaustion I felt just pushing my upper body to a sitting position. By the time I grabbed the crutches that the therapist handed to me, I was already breaking a sweat. At that point, I felt confident enough to start pulling myself up from the edge of the bed, but when I saw my wife and daughter looking at me with such concern in their eyes, I understood that I wasn't looking good at all.

The sharp pain going through my hips and shoulder was holding me down, but I didn't want to give up. I took a deep breath, and gradually, I started to pull myself up. Once I was up and getting ready to take my first step, the therapist positioned himself next to me in case I lost my strength. I took my first step very slowly, and as I continued with a few more baby steps in the same slow motion, suddenly I could feel my body wanting to collapse on the floor. I tried to turn around, but without the help from the therapist, I was certainly not able to get back into the bed, where I remained until the next day, when I had to do it again.

The following day, I was able to pass their minimum requirements on my own, and I was glad that we didn't have to spend another day in the hospital, but I certainly wasn't looking to the ride back home since we had to drive our car.

Chapter 5

Thankfully, Natali crafted the passenger seat into a bed by extending the back seat to allow me enough room to stretch out so I wouldn't put too much weight on my pelvic area. But even with all that effort, I could still feel pain at every turn the car took, every stop, every bump, and every change in lanes. On top of that, I knew I had to take about twenty steps to get upstairs into our apartment once we got home, and I couldn't allow anybody to help me because I had to control my body in a way that was comfortable for me. But once I finally made it to the top of the stairs, I went straight to our bedroom and remained there.

Natali brought Bella back home from the PetSmart hotel the following morning, and we were all very excited to see her. Normally, when she saw me, she would run toward me, but that day she approached me with sharp-eyed caution, and her nose sniffed suspiciously like she was on a discovery mission. Her tail was wagging wildly, but her energy level remained calm. She looked at me as if she knew something was wrong, and amazingly, she remained quiet and still around me the entire time.

My days started to feel much longer, the nights felt like they would never end, and my entire body began to ache because of the constant lying flat on my back in bed. The lack of movement and exercise weakened me, and my muscles were shrinking too. I started to wake up a lot at night, and because I couldn't go back to sleep easily, I decided the best thing to do would be to move to the living room. That way, I wouldn't disturb Natali.

The living room couch wasn't a sofa sleeper, so Natali moved the bed from the guest room into the living room to make me more comfortable. And as soon as everything was set for me, Bella claimed her side of the bed.

I don't know if she believed that the bed was brought there just for her, but I absolutely know that she could definitely win a prize for being the biggest cuddler in the world since she never wanted to leave my side, and for that, I appreciated her more!

I truly expected, as time passed, that I would get to a much better state of mind, but when I still couldn't sleep well and I could feel my body weaken day after day, my frustration started to grow, which led me into a mild depression. I kept trying to occupy my mind by watching all kinds of TV shows and movies, but after about a week, TV was no longer distracting me, so I needed to find something else.

I did have a project that I wanted to start working on for quite a while, but I never had the time to start doing it since it required a lot of time and research to do. But with the situation I got myself into, I didn't have any excuse not to start working on it, plus I hoped that all the research I would need to start writing the novel that I had in my head, based on true historical events, would definitely help distract me from my pain and pull me out of my depression.

Natali brought me a ton of books from the library, and I started reading and writing like I never did before. The days were flying by quickly, and eventually, my depression faded away.

I already knew that I enjoyed working on projects that requires imagination and creativity, but writing was giving me a totally different feeling and a very unique satisfaction that I hadn't yet felt in my life. Every moment spent and each word I added to the story helped me realize that I didn't just enjoy writing—it allowed me to discover the passion that I never knew I had inside of me for writing. My days became much more enjoyable because of it, and from that moment, I hoped that one day writing stories would become a big part of my life.

A few weeks later, I was able to start walking around the apartment using my crutches, walks that felt like small parades as my family would stop and just watch me walk.

Bella was staring at me with confusion in her eyes but also curiosity because she couldn't figure out if my slow motion meant playtime or something else. My daughter would always ask if I needed anything or if she could help me with something, while my wife just stared at me happily, noticing that I was getting better.

It felt extremely good to be able to move around again, and once I felt more confident on my feet, I started walking outside of the apartment. I was still using the crutches, but the more I walked, the faster I could get rid of them.

Then finally, three months after my accident, the doctor that I was referred to from the hospital to follow up with my recovery allowed me to start doing all the things I used to do before the accident and start driving again.

I was relieved to know that I could go back to work even if I wasn't able to work as much as before since driving for more than three hours would bring a numbing sensation of my midsection. But I was happy to have any money coming in since the bills from the hospital were piling up on top of our regular bills.

In the meantime, on one of our daily family walks around the neighborhood, we ran into an old friend of Natali's that I hadn't met, and they hadn't even seen each other for more than ten years. He was a sergeant on the police department from our city, and after a long, pleasant conversation with him, he mentioned that the department was hiring.

The information immediately sparked my interest despite the fact that I wasn't ready physically at all. Plus, there wasn't much time to gather all the necessary paperwork to register, knowing that the registration deadline was noon on that coming Monday and we met on Friday evening.

However, as we were walking back home, I decided to apply for the position of a police officer once again. So after I successfully gathered all the required documents by Sunday night, I had Natali drop it off first thing in the morning, and from that time, I had four weeks to train for the physical exam.

It seemed impossible to get myself ready in such a short period, considering that just a month and a half ago I started walking again without crutches, and my injury dropped my body weight from 190 pounds to 155 pounds, which was a loss of a lot of muscle mass, plus my power was not the same. But I refused to believe that I couldn't do it, and I started to train as hard as I could.

I was already doing some light exercises at home, but once I began to exercise outside with Bella, running, jumping over various obstacles in the park, and swimming in the lake like we used to do, it all got me back into shape faster than I was expecting. She definitely was one of the puzzle pieces in my improvement and the extra motivator that helped speed up my training, but together with the help of my wife's many stretching sessions and my daughter's moral support, I proudly passed the physical exam and the written test. And that instantly put me on the new-hire waiting list.

I couldn't have been more proud of myself for working that hard to make it on that list, but I certainly refused to get too excited since the last time I tried to apply for the Chicago Police Department I unexpectedly received disappointing news. So I continued with my life like nothing important had happened.

I continued driving for a living, spent as much time as I could with all three of my girls since all of them needed a lot of attention from me, and then when I had some extra time for myself, I happily continued working on the novel that I started to write.

I wished I had as much time as I wanted to write, but with the increased hours at work, along with waking up very early, my writing time was extremely limited. What's more, I couldn't change much since I was the only one making money for our family.

In the meantime, I successfully passed the police department's psychological exam, as well the polygraph test, and that meant it was just a matter of time until I would receive the letter for the next exam.

That year, my daughter already turned five years old, and we couldn't believe it was time for her to go to kindergarten. There were some schools around our area, but after going to a few orientations, we decided to register her at a Catholic school that was connected to a Catholic church. We liked the idea to have her there because she could attend that same school all the way through eighth grade, and since it was just a ten-minute walk from our home, we could easily drop her off there and then walk to pick her up from there as well. But what I liked the most was that she could have a similar upbringing as I did when I was growing up.

As a child, I was raised by my parents as well as one of my grandaunts who had lived with us until I was ten years old. My grandaunt never had any children of her own, so she took care of me as if I were her own son. She was a very religious person who went to church very often, and because I spent a lot of time with her, church also became a part of my life growing up. It taught me about love and kindness. It introduced me to a lot of friends, and I learned that the time spent together with family is the most important thing in the world. I liked everything about it, and I wanted the same for my daughter. And as soon as the school year started, my daughter was super excited for her next day, which truly pleased us about choosing that school.

She loved her new teacher and easily made new friends, especially with Bella taking Sydney to school or picking her up. All Bella had to do was wag her tail and smile, and she would instantly be surrounded by a wall of children who wanted to pet her and say hello. Without a doubt, Bella made it extra simple for Sydney to make friends, but if Sydney needed protection, Bella was ready for that, too, no matter who it was.

She would even position herself in between Sydney and my wife or me when Sydney would get in trouble or get lectured, and she would just stand guard and watch us. And it definitely helped Sydney out every time because it shortened the lecture since it was impossible to stay mad when we saw their adorable facial expressions, just waiting for us to "get over it."

As for the hiring process for the police department, I had one more exam before I decided to go on a few ride-along. That way, I could observe and get more direct knowledge about the job and absolutely get a better feel for it.

I was able to witness someone get arrested for possession of and playing with a knife in a public place. I watched two teenagers get caught drinking alcohol in the back seat of their friend's car while he was driving. I took part as a spectator in a domestic call and also to a shooting call related to some gang activity. And after witnessing all that in such a short period, I absolutely had a better understanding and a better feeling about this job I wanted.

Sooner than I expected, I was scheduled for the very last exam in the hiring process that I successfully passed, and then at the end of the year, I was hired and proudly sworn in along with three other candidates.

I could never forget the day I was given my badge and swore the oath of a police officer. It's a dramatic moment in any police officer's life because the badge stands for everything that is good and just, and they will die in the name of that badge and what it stands for and treasure it for the rest of their lives.

I was very proud of myself for completing the hiring process and to finally get my turn to start the police academy, but as I completed the oath and saw my wife holding my daughter in her arms, watching me from the auditorium, I realized that my life would never be the same. Lots of mixed emotions started to arise inside of my head. I wanted to open up about the way I was feeling with my family, but since I didn't even know what I was dealing with, I decided to keep it to myself. Then there were the things that started happening throughout the police departments across the United States right before I was supposed to start the police academy.

Sadly, two innocent police officers who were just sitting in their patrol car were tragically shot at point-blank range, killed by a man who officials said had traveled there just to kill police officers. And that happened at a moment when huge protests over police tactics had already agitated parts of the nation and police brutality was a hot topic that could be seen everywhere in the media.

People were turning against the police, and to see the photo that the killer posted online before he murdered the two innocent police officers with comments like "I'm Putting Wings On Pigs Today. They Take 1 Of Ours . . . Let's Take 2 of Theirs and #ShootThePolice" was not only breaking my heart but also messing with my head.

I was supposed to be happy to start working as a police officer, but instead, there I was at five o'clock in the morning on the first day of the police academy, dressed in a suit, waiting in the parking lot inside of my car, thinking of my family and asking myself, "What am I really doing here?"

That morning, all the cadets were supposed to wait in the parking lot until our assigned instructors came outside to give us the next instructions, and not one cadet was waiting outside of their car because of the bitter temperature. It was very cold. The ground was covered with ice, and snow had started to fall.

Once we were taken inside the gymnasium, they checked us all for the mandatory gear we were supposed to have with us. If someone was missing any of the required items, they were definitely punished by doing push-ups and running laps even though they were dressed in suits and tie with dressy shoes. And then if someone didn't follow the orders they were given, all of us would have to start doing push-ups and run laps.

I personally expected something else from the first day of the academy, and the constant reminder throughout the day about things changing for police and that police now have targets on their backs started to give me lots to think about.

Back in 2006, when I applied for a job with the Chicago Police, I was twenty-six years old and a bit wilder. I wasn't that worried about the danger that would come with the job and didn't care to analyze it. But nine years later, with more life experience and becoming a father, my subconscious began to consider everything from my life, reminding me about the promise that I made to myself after the snowboarding accident. So I listened to how I felt, and I kept my promise to myself and decided not to continue with the police academy.

It wasn't an easy decision to resign, knowing that many people might think less of me when they found out that I dropped out of the police academy, but I did it, and I was proud that I tried what I believed would be good for me and my family. And after seeing how far I came, I had certainly learned that everything is possible as long as we try and believe in it.

Luckily, nobody bought my semitruck, which was up for sale since the day I was sworn in to the police department, so I called the owner of the company I used to work with to check if I could work again with them. After explaining the situation I was in, he was happy to have me back, and the next week, I started driving again.

And just as I expected, many people I knew were very surprised about my decision. Some people had no problem sharing their honest opinion, telling me that if they had been in my position they would never have quit even though they couldn't understand how I felt or they would never try anything like that. But other people totally understood and respected the decision I made.

Learning more about myself through that experience made me want to cut some of my driving hours so I could open up some time for me to try to pursue writing, and I did a month after I quit the academy. Unfortunately, that extra time I carved out would suddenly need to be devoted to finding another place to live when, unexpectedly, our landlord needed the apartment we were living in for family reasons.

We totally understood, but we couldn't believe that we were given just two months to find another place, knowing that we might have difficulties again finding rentals that would allow us to bring our dog, Bella, again, because of her breed.

It was the beginning of March when I started to search for available apartments around the same area we lived, hoping that we could still take our daughter to the same school. Just about ten years had passed since we last tried to find an apartment that allowed Bella's pit bull breed to live in a pet-friendly apartment, and sadly, nothing had changed. Our applications were still turned down because of her breed, and the more we looked, the more rejections we found.

We couldn't just give up since we had to move out, so we needed to enlist a realtor to help us out. Luckily, a few days later, he found an available two-bedroom apartment in a two-flat building just ten minutes away from where we lived without any pet restrictions. The rent was more expensive, but at that point, we didn't have any other option. The realtor made an appointment with the agency handling the rental, and we went to check it out.

While looking through the apartment, suddenly I heard a woman's voice by the front door.

"Hello? Who's there?" she asked with some concern in her tone.

Nobody else should have been in the apartment, so I started to be suspicious as well. Whoever was on the other side of the door definitely realized that someone was in the building, because we parked our car right in the driveway.

"Hello? We are here to check out the apartment for rent," I answered as I was walking toward the front entrance.

The door slowly opened, and an elderly woman cautiously entered the room to find out who might be in the apartment. She was the owner of the building, and she lived in the apartment above. Because she wasn't notified about our appointment, she was worried about who was there since there was a lock with a code in order to enter the apartment.

She seemed like a very nice lady in her mid-seventies. We found out that she lost the love of her life a few years back, and maintaining a two-flat apartment building wasn't easy to do on her own. She didn't want to sell it, but in order to keep up with her bills and the maintenance, she decided that the best solution was to rent one of the apartments in her building.

We told her about us and that we had another family member at home who was a nine-and-a-half-year-old pit bull mix, and she didn't mind at all. She really seemed to like us, and she said that we could move in at the end of the month if we would want.

Since she shared the reason why she had to rent the apartment, I even offered to do the outdoor work around the building at no cost. She seemed very relieved to take my offer, and it appeared as if everything would work out for us. She did mention that she had a showing for the apartment later that day, but she told us not to worry about it because she wanted to have us there.

We still had to send the application to the rental agency she was working with in order for them to get their commission, but beside that, we just had to wait to receive the approval confirmation. And then we could pay the security deposit and move in.

The application was sent by our realtor on the same day, but two days later, we received an unanticipated denial for our application. The lady changed her mind about having us live there, and she decided to take the couple that looked at the apartment later that same day. Supposedly, they didn't have a dog. That's what we were told by our realtor.

We were very disappointed with what happened, but we couldn't stop looking for a new place to rent. We were even thinking of buying something, but the time we had left was way too short to find something that we would love. So renting still remained our only option. And since we weren't finding anything around our area that allowed us to bring Bella, we had to admit to ourselves that we'd have to move even further than we wanted.

Without any pet-friendly options for apartment rentals, we needed to try to rent houses as well, also meaning that we would spend a lot more money, but it still didn't matter because Bella's breed was still killing our chance for approval.

The situation became very stressful for us, and we truly started to feel that we couldn't get anywhere. Some people who knew about our situation even very honestly told us to just give the dog away and we could move anywhere we want without going through all that drama. Of course, those people were the kind of people who never had a pet in their entire life, and they can't understand the indescribable love and attachment you can have with your dog.

It was undeniable that our situation was very stressful for us, but the endless love that Bella had for us, the way she made us smile every single day, the way she could bring back our happiness on some stressful days, and the feeling of safety and protection she gave our family made her a unique family member. She absolutely carved her name on my heart from the very first second our eyes met at the shelter, and she was definitely staying in our family until the end of her life. On the other hand, Bella was definitely not the problem. We could only blame the people that judged dogs just by their breed or looks and nothing else.

We were already at the end of April, and we still couldn't find any apartments or houses that allowed us to move in with Bella. Then we finally came across an ad for a large newly built apartment complex that stated, "Dogs and cats okay," nothing else. The ad didn't specify anything about pet restrictions, so my wife called them right away to ask about the availability of the apartment. She didn't bring up anything about Bella's breed.

It sounded like we finally found a place until the dreaded question "What kind of dog do you have?" popped into the conversation. As soon as my wife said a pit bull mix, she was immediately interrupted by the lady from the other end of the phone with a disappointing and the usual response: "We're sorry, but we don't allow pit bulls . . ."

We were sick and tired of hearing that all the time, and my wife didn't have the patience to wait for the lady to finish explaining anything else when she snapped all of a sudden, which wasn't something my wife would normally do.

"You judge a dog by their breed, and you don't even know my dog. Why don't you ask what kind of temperament my dog has, or have a test that allows my dog to prove its character and personality? Or even better, allow our vet, neighbors, friends, and family to vouch for her lovable and calm demeanor! Dogs can't speak for themselves, and what you are doing is wrong, and it is prejudice against a breed, and you should be very ashamed of that!"

My wife was so fired up that she even used two big influential celebrity names during the conversation. She said that she would even try to get ahold of both of them to shine a spotlight on the breedism that already exists. Then she ended the conversation by saying, "You can write down my name and phone number because you will definitely hear from me again!"

And unbelievably, my wife received a phone call the next day from the same lady from that apartment complex. She asked if we would like to send her a couple of pictures of our dog with a letter from our veterinarian describing Bella, because they might consider allowing us to rent one of their apartments.

We believe they didn't change their minds for the love of animals. It was more likely that the lady was worried when my wife mentioned the two very influential people that have their own television show, and they probably didn't want to take any chances that they might find themselves getting bad advertising for their newly opened apartment complex. We wouldn't feel genuinely welcome there even if everything would work out perfectly, so we decided not to fill out the paperwork.

We spoke to our landlord about our situation, and she kindly allowed us to stay for another month while we continued to fill out application after application even though we knew what to expect. But we couldn't lose hope, knowing that we had four weeks left before we had to move out.

It was phone call after phone call, application after application, until I found another potential landlord who apparently didn't care about the breed of our dog. Plus, it sounded too good to be true, especially knowing that the rental was also part of an association. The rent would cost twice as much as what we were paying, but once we met with the owner and realized that the association did not have anything against pit bulls, I quickly said, "We'll take it," without asking any questions or carefully inspecting the inside of the townhouse.

The owner looked very shocked at my quick decision, but he didn't know the stress we had to go through until we found that townhouse. And to make sure that we would have the deal locked in, I met with him again later that day to sign the one-year contract and give him the required security deposit. And then we could move in and finally be able to breathe easily even though things had to change for all of us.

Sydney would have to start first grade in a new school and try to make new friends. My wife and I would have to say goodbye to some really good neighbors we got to know during the past ten years. But the biggest and most painful change was leaving behind all our family memories with Sydney and Bella growing up in that area.

The stress that I accumulated while trying to get our new place would be difficult for me to describe, and I certainly didn't want to go through something like that again. So I decided that during our stay in the new place we would hunt for a house, and when we would find something that we loved that was affordable, we would try to buy it.

Chapter 6

We moved out at the end of May, and Sydney's transition into the new home was very smooth. She liked her new teacher, and she made new friends at school and around our neighborhood easily. She also started gymnastics outside of school that we registered her for, and she loved it.

As for Bella, since she always loved to run and play fetch without taking a break, we managed to find a spot where we could go play and throw the ball for her like we did in the old neighborhood. But not too long after we moved into the new house, we noticed that she was becoming sorer after chasing the ball than before.

Considering that Bella was ten years old, we thought her age might be the reason for her soreness, but as winter approached us with its colder temperatures, Bella's soreness after fetching the ball outside seemed to get much worse. There were times that Sydney feed Bella from her hands because Bella refused to even stand up from her bed to go eat—that's how sore she was.

So we decided to take a break from running and playing fetch with her and only take her for short walks to see if she would feel better, which worked. Bella seemed much better, but we decided to have her wait to play fetch for a little longer even though she was desperately asking for more playtimes. That way, we could find out for sure if that was the cause of her soreness.

For the time being, we kept searching for houses, but I didn't think it would be so hard to find something that we liked that would also be reasonably priced. There were plenty of houses to choose from, but many of them didn't look anything like they did in the listing when we showed up to see them in person. They were totally different-looking than what we expected, and all the problems could not be hidden like they were in the pictures. But by the middle of November, I came across another available house for sale that was brand-new on the market that caught my attention. It was approximately fifteen minutes away from where we lived. Its location was wonderful for us, and the school assigned to that address was great.

Since we weren't working with an agent at that time, I called the listing agent to schedule a showing. And after viewing the property we were very content with everything we saw even though I realized that the house needed some updates. But I could see potential, and I knew we could do most of the work for remodeling, so we put in an offer on the house.

Once they accepted our offer, we tried to push for the closing to happen before the holidays so we could move into our new house before Christmas. But since I was self-employed, the bank started to request some extra paperwork from me, and the closing date for the house had to be postponed until after the holidays. We weren't given any particular date; we just had to wait until the paperwork would clear out.

The news disappointed us, but it didn't ruin our holiday. We still had a beautiful Christmas and New Year's Eve full of snow and fun and activities. But once again playing outside in the snow with Bella, we realized that she was getting sore again and started to limp. And that time, we didn't even play as long as we used to play.

Usually, the soreness would disappear and she would be back to normal activities within a few days, but that time, more than a week had passed by; and instead of getting better, she was getting worse. It seemed like she was having a lot of discomfort around her front right shoulder joint.

As we tried to gently massage her, we could feel a swollen area near the shoulder joint, and it seemed as if that might be the cause of her soreness. So we called to make an appointment with the veterinarian who had known Bella since she was a puppy. After a quick examination, supposedly the swollen area was just another fat pocket.

Bella had a surgery for a fat pocket removal before, but this time, scheduling surgery to remove it wasn't necessary since the lump was not that obvious. The vet gave us some medicine for her and told us to make her rest as much as possible with minimal activity.

We stopped playing with her outside and took her for short walks just enough to do her business, but watching her walk in pain toward her basket with toys to bring us a ball so we could throw it for her was painful for us as well since we couldn't do it. She didn't understand why we didn't want to throw the ball; and to see the disappointment in her eyes while going back and forth to my wife, my daughter, and me, trying to make us understand that she really wanted to play, was even more painful. But because she always ended up on someone's lap, she would forget about the ball, and she would just lie there happily.

Meanwhile, we received news about the closing date for the house, and the paperwork was ready to be signed. That was very good news, but it was difficult to enjoy knowing that we had to figure out what was going on with Bella since she wasn't getting any better. The swelling on the right side of her chest became enlarged, very visible, and it started to create such discomfort for her that she couldn't stand or walk on her front right leg.

The medicine that she received for her joints didn't seem to work any longer, so we scheduled an appointment with a different vet who had an office near our home. She believed it was necessary to perform a few tests and extract some cells from the fat lump on Bella to get a complete diagnosis.

We didn't want to believe that Bella might have anything worse than a fat pocket or muscle soreness, but we wanted the best for her, so we agreed to have all the necessary tests done. We prayed to receive only good news, and two days later, we were ready to find out if our prayers were heard when the veterinarian called me first thing in the morning.

She told me that she tried to reach my wife first, but the phone calls were going straight to her voice mail and she didn't want to leave a message. She said she had Bella's test results, but unfortunately, they didn't look good.

My heart was already sinking in my chest, trying to hide from the pain of what was coming next. Then when she continued to tell me that regrettably Bella had cancer cells and they've already spread throughout her entire body, before I knew it, I could feel tears flooding my eyes. The vet started to explain to me our options for Bella's treatment, but I couldn't focus on the conversation any longer, so I told her that I would call her later to talk about it.

Immediately after I hung up with her, I called my wife, but I also kept getting her voice mail. I tried calling her several times before I sent her a text asking to call me back when she had a chance. That morning, she dropped Sydney off at school, and while shopping for some groceries, her phone battery died. But as soon as she arrived home, she called me.

It was extremely hard for me to give her the bad news over the phone, knowing that she would be devastated, and just as expected, as soon as I started to explain to her what the vet said to me, she started crying. And I couldn't think of anything else to say to ease her pain. I was at a loss for words, and I just sat frozen and quiet with tears in my eyes, listening to her cry. As she lay down next to Bella and pulled her toward her chest, Bella started to lick the flooding tears from my wife's eyes as she was trying to tell her that everything would be all right.

Once I arrived home, we called the vet to ask about the treatment options for Bella, but since the cancer cells had already spread throughout her entire body, the only option they offered was chemotherapy. Unbelievably, Bella was already in an advanced phase of cancer, and there wasn't too much that could be done besides start the process that would probably last just as long as her body could resist. Without a doubt, we wanted what was best for Bella, but we couldn't lie to ourselves also that if we chose chemotherapy for her, in her condition it would be a very selfish way of keeping her with us. And the last thing that we wanted was to see our sweet dog endure even more pain.

Once we closed on the house, we had to start working on some of the projects that needed to be done before we moved in—things like painting the bedrooms, refinishing the hardwood floor, and replacing the carpet. I tried to complete those projects after work and on weekends, and with Natali helping every day after she dropped Sydney off at school, things were moving along quickly.

We brought Bella there with us every time we went, but it was heartbreaking to see her just lie on her bed, not able to roam around and sniff every corner of our new house or run around in our backyard with Sydney. Her health was going downhill more and more every day, and we tried to spend as much time with her as we could, knowing that our story together might be coming to an end soon.

Sydney didn't even know the truth about Bella's health since we didn't exactly know how to explain to a six-year-old that her sister would soon be missing from our family. But with Bella's health getting much worse, it was also impossible to keep hiding it from her. Bella's right front shoulder became twice as big as the left shoulder, and the tumor already spread into her back legs, forcing her to drag her left leg on the floor. That meant she couldn't even go outside to take care of her business without our help.

Even though we did buy some medicine to relieve her pain, it didn't take any pain from our hearts when we observed our sweet dog dying from that malicious tumor right in front of our eyes. And seeing her like that, we knew we had to stop lying to ourselves that she might get better.

We were all suffering, and we all knew there wasn't a good time to say to someone that you truly love your last goodbye, give your last kiss, or give your very last hug; but since Easter was just one week away, we truly believed that was a blessed time for her beautiful soul to make its way to heaven. So with lots of love and lots of pain in our hearts, we spoke with her vet about our decision to put our Bella to her eternal sleep on Good Friday.

There wasn't a single day when I returned from work when my heart and my eyes desperately wanted to see Bella waiting for me by the window like she used to before her health collapsed. She always knew about my arrival way before I would pull my car up to our garage, and as soon as I would open the front door, tidal waves of kisses were expected from her. And then of course, she would intensely sniff at my shoes and clothing as if she were investigating the places I had been that day. But unfortunately, that had vanished along with her health, and sadly, our last day together had arrived.

I knew that the work I had on that fateful day would take me around five hours, so I woke up at two o'clock in the morning to be back home by the time everyone would be awake. Luckily, I didn't experience any problems on the road, and I had finished my work for the day by 9:30 a.m., and by 10:30 a.m., I was back home. I was still praying for a miracle that when I would open the front door Bella would run to me just like before, but once I opened the door and saw my wife with my daughter just lying on the floor next to Bella, I realized that no miracle would happen.

As I was taking off my shoes so I could go and say hello to my girls, Bella's tail started to wag, and she slowly tried to stand up to come to me. The look in her eyes seemed like she was trying desperately to recapture her former liveliness. I got down on my knees, and with my arms wide open, I said to her, "Come on, sweetie! Do you want to come here?"

And then she started walking toward me as if nothing was wrong with her until sadly after only a few steps her legs gave up on her, forcing her to collapse. I immediately picked her up and took her back to her bed, where Natali, Sydney, and I stayed until it was time to go to the vet.

Yet again, we tried our best to explain to our six-year-old daughter that her sister Bella would no longer be with us after the trip to the vet, but we could tell that she didn't really fully understand the situation.

The fateful hour had arrived. My wife and I already had tears flooding our eyes, but as soon as I picked Bella up from her bed to take her to the car, Natali's eyes couldn't hold its tears any longer. My body was aching to release the pain, too, but for some reason, I couldn't cry with my daughter there. And watching her gently pet Bella on her head, telling her everything would be all right, just made it more difficult for me to keep my tears inside.

Once we arrived at the vet's office, we checked in at the front desk, and then we were led to a small room that supposedly was also the room where we would see Bella for our very last time. We all sat down with Bella on the floor and started to give her kisses when we heard three knocks on the door, and the door opened. It was the vet. She came to explain to us the two shots that Bella would get to end her pain forever, and after that, she asked us if we needed a little more time with Bella before she would begin the procedure.

We didn't want to have just a little more time with Bella. We wanted to have our entire lifetime with her. As we hung out on the floor with her to shower her with more kisses and hugs, ten minutes passed by like the blink of an eye; and before we knew it, the vet was back in our room with two syringes in her hand. The first shot was to calm Bella down and put her into a deep sleep while the second shot would stop her heart.

Natali took Bella on her lap while I held Sydney in my arms. The vet got down on one knee next to Bella, and after a gentle pat on her head, she gave her the first shot. Then she left the room. At that moment, Natali burst out crying as she pulled Bella as close to her chest as she could while my daughter looked at me, confused, and whispered into my ear, "Why is Mommy crying so hard?"

As a man and as a father, I thought I needed to stay strong in that situation even though my heart was screaming in pain.

"Mommy is crying so hard because she loves Bella very much," I said to her, not knowing what else I could tell her.

But as I watched Bella fading into a deep sleep and Sydney asked me as she looked into my eyes, "So why don't you cry then, Daddy? You love her too," my eyes couldn't stay dry any longer, and I couldn't hide the emotions I kept bottled up. And Sydney only needed to see my first tear fall before her sweet eyes became flooded with tears of love for our dog too.

By the time the vet came back in the room with the second shot, Bella was already in a deep sleep, and our tears continued to flow, knowing what would happen next. The vet gave us all a hug, and after she checked if Bella was fully asleep, she gave her the second shot. Then she stood up, and after telling us that we made the best decision for Bella and to take as much time as we needed to say our last goodbyes, she left the room.

Slowly Bella stopped breathing, and her body became heavy and limp. Her tongue fell out of her mouth as if she were hot and needed some water, and sweet Sydney was trying to push it back inside of her mouth.

"Mommy, why isn't Bella moving anymore?" she asked without realizing yet what was really happening with our precious Bella.

"Because Bella is an angel now, sweetheart," replied Natali as she took Bella's ears into her hands, showing Sydney the pink color vanishing and turning to white, resembling angel wings on Bella's head. Sydney put her hands on Bella's "angel wings" and started sobbing so hard that we were concerned she might pass out.

We all couldn't take our eyes off Bella, and it was extremely difficult to leave her behind in that room, but we gave her one last kiss and went back home.

Our hope was that packing our stuff for the move into our new house would be enough of a distraction to help us emotionally, but going through Bella's stuff didn't make it easier. All our memories together were coming back, and getting rid of anything Bella had was impossible. So we decided to pack it up and keep it for as long as we felt we needed to have it.

Chapter 7

After Easter weekend, we started moving into our new house, and by the end of the week, we had everything moved in and ready to unpack. Without Bella around, everything seemed very quiet, and we still couldn't get used to the idea of her being gone. Her presence was so missed from our family that my wife and my daughter already began asking for a new puppy.

Personally, I was still very angry and saddened that Bella was taken from our family that quickly, so my heart was definitely not ready for another puppy. I refused to even talk about it. Besides, the way Bella was taken away from us after what we went through as a family for her, I absolutely didn't want to get another puppy. I just wanted Bella back. And since the house still had a lot of projects to be finished, the thought of getting a new puppy remained my last concern.

However, with the summer around the corner, the inside of the house was finally coming along nicely, so we were happy to spend more time outside of the house. Sydney enjoyed playing with friends, chasing one another through our backyard. She started making new friends around the neighborhood, and to see her smile again was a blessing for us—she definitely needed that.

Yet the more fun we had together, the more we thought about our four-legged friend, and Natali with my daughter started to beg me again for a puppy even though we agreed that we would wait for the right time. Plus, with plenty of projects left to do around the house I knew that I wouldn't have much free time to enjoy playing and watch the puppy grow, which would also be unfair for me.

They did listen to what I had to say, but their birthdays were coming up, and since their birthdays were only two days apart, they still tried using that as leverage to get a puppy. And boy, were they laying it on thick! They said to me, "We know that you have to spend a lot of money to finish all these house projects, so we would definitely be happy to have just one gift for the both of us that we can share with each other."

They certainly weren't shy about repeating their wish every time they had a chance prior to their birthdays, but I still managed to keep our agreement that we originally made as a family about waiting to get a new puppy at the right time.

So my daughter didn't get a puppy for her birthday, but she was elated to have a big party with a bunch of her friends in our backyard. And the large bouncy house that I rented as one of her gifts definitely helped her forget about her real request.

On the other hand, my wife was not that pleased with her gift since there wasn't a puppy jumping out of a gift box I had for her, and she decided to begin sending me many text messages with pictures of puppies that were in need of a home. She only used rescue websites, and her search criteria were already narrowed down so she would exclusively receive adoption updates for puppies that were a female pit bull mix, similar to Bella. And there were so many puppies ready to be adopted that I would get picture after picture. And then when she didn't send me texts, she would wait until bedtime to show me some more pictures.

But despite the fact that many of those puppies' faces were extremely adorable that numerous times I almost gave in, something still held me back—I couldn't give in yet. I was still disappointed by the fact that after we worked so hard to remain a family and finally got the house where Bella would be unquestionably welcomed unlike nearly all of the rentals that wouldn't accept her for her breed, she was still taken away from us.

There was no way I could have known the reason why it happened like that, but I definitely knew that we were missing her very much. And when we needed to refresh our memories of her, we would flip through the many pictures we had of her in our family albums, like we did on September 21, 2016—an extraordinary day that I will always remember as if it had happened yesterday.

I was on my way home from work when all of a sudden it started drizzling. It wasn't that cloudy, but by the time I arrived home, the sky was already changing color. As soon as I opened the front, unexpectedly my daughter jumped into my arms and gave me a huge hug. She kissed me on my cheek, and then she jumped down and ran toward the living room. She looked happy, but her eyes were kind of glossy. I took off my shoes, and as soon as I entered the living room, I saw my wife sitting at the dining room table with our entire collection of family photo albums. My daughter asked me if I would like to look at pictures with them, so I sat down at the table and began to enjoy the many nice memories our family had together.

The sky became much darker, and we could hear some thunder in the distance. By the time we were looking through the third photo album, the thunder seemed much closer to us, lights were flashing through the sky, and buckets of rain were pouring down.

Much to my disbelief, my wife asked if we wanted to go upstairs to relax on the carpet and watch the storm from the big windows. I was shocked, to say the least, by her request since they were frightened of lightning storms ever since they witnessed lightning strike our window in the apartment where we used to live. But I looked at my daughter, and to my surprise, she agreed. So we left the photo albums on the table and went upstairs where we lay down on the carpet in front of the big windows that faced the golf course across from our house.

An earsplitting bang grabbed our attention, and a gigantic lightning bolt pierced the dark clouds. That reminded Sydney of the day when she was watching cartoons with my wife and Bella in our old apartment and lightning struck the window, so she quickly snuggled up tight next to me.

"Daddy, I am very afraid of lightning," she said as she tried to build herself a body shield with my arms.

"You shouldn't be afraid of lightning," I said to her.

Then I felt a need inside me to make up a story for her fear of lightning to go away. So as soon as I asked her if she wanted me to tell her a story, she became all ears.

And I began . . .

"The story I'm about to tell you is called 'The Furry Sister.' Once upon a time, on a hot summer day, a beautiful little girl was born. Sydney was the name that was given to her by her parents, and they couldn't have been happier to have another girl in their life."

As soon as I said "Sydney," my daughter's eyes lit up, and she became more intrigued to listen to what was coming next since she was part of the story. So I continued . . .

"Of course, Sydney was way too young to realize what was going on in her life since the only thing she did was sleep, eat, sleep, and eat again. But the more time passed, the more aware she became of her surroundings and the more curious she became. And what she was the most curious to discover was to find out who was constantly licking her fingers from underneath the table every time she ate.

"Sydney thought she knew at least the name of the finger licker from underneath the table, but she was absolutely incorrect. Nobella was certainly not the name. Sydney's parents were just saying, 'No, Bella!' to their dog, whose name was only Bella, trying to discipline and train her to leave Sydney alone while she ate, because Bella always tried to eat Sydney's food. But Sydney didn't mind at all that. She even began to sneak Bella food every time she had a chance when she wouldn't be caught, and that made them the best of friends.

"One day, as they were playing outside having fun, chasing each other, a very loud sound was heard in the distance from the sky that instantly made them stop running. They looked up, and humongous dark clouds with flashing lights flying through the sky were coming toward them at the speed of light. Sydney was mesmerized by the image she could see in the sky, but when a loud thunder shook the ground under her feet, she became frightened. 'Let's go home!' she yelled to Bella as she started running toward the house, where their mom was already waiting for them with the front door wide open. The sky became black as night, rain started pouring down, and a competition between the loudest thunder began.

"They all went inside of the house, and while they waited for the bad weather to fade away, they decided to get comfortable on the living room couch and watch some cartoons on TV. But the weather seemed as if it were getting worse by the minute instead of fading away, and the thunder became much louder. Flashes of lightning were seen everywhere.

"Sydney, Bella, and their mom started to get anxious, so they began to cuddle as close as they could to each other on the couch when suddenly an ear-deafening pop struck the window frame in the same room where they were watching cartoons.

"The TV instantaneously turned off, and smoke was coming out from the window frame. Sydney and Bella jumped off immediately of the couch and ran into her room to hide underneath the bed while their mom remained on the couch in disbelief, watching the window that just got struck by lightning, making sure a fire wouldn't start.

"Since then, Sydney was terrified of lightning, and every time bad weather would occur, she would always hide underneath her bed. But Bella would always be next to her, trying to make her feel safe, and she wouldn't leave Sydney's side until the bad weather would pass. Their bond grew stronger as time passed. Their love for each other was unlike any other, and Bella was no longer just Sydney's best friend. Bella had become Sydney's best furry sister. They became inseparable, and everywhere they were, laughter could be heard.

"But sadly, their life together had to come to an end when unexpectedly Bella got very sick, and unfortunately, nobody could do anything to save her. And very soon, Bella wasn't with her family any longer, which made Sydney miss her very much, especially when bad weather would occur, and Sydney would hide underneath her bed scared.

"However, Sydney's furry sister never stopped watching over her from the sky, especially on the stormy days when she knew that Sydney would be hiding underneath her bed scared and lonely. But the more she watched Sydney, the guiltier Bella felt that she couldn't be there for her.

"Sydney's parents also felt sad watching their daughter go to her bedroom and hide underneath her bed every time bad weather would occur. So on a very stormy summer day with lots of rain, loud thunder, and flashes of lightning, they decided to take Sydney from underneath her bed and watch together from inside their home the beautiful display that the summer storm created, hoping that would help Sydney with her fear of lightning.

"Surprisingly, Sydney agreed to do it, but as soon as they started to watch the weather through the windows that overlooked the golf course across from their house, Sydney's parents mysteriously fell asleep. Suddenly, Sydney heard a thunder as loud as an explosion, and right after that, she saw a marvelous lightning bolt that pierced the dark sky. Shockingly, the loud thunder didn't wake her parents, and they seemed as if they were in a deeper sleep than usual.

"Sydney looked back outside, and then she realized that everything froze for a second. Nothing was moving. It was very quiet, and she was able to see each and every drop of rain with its very different size just floating in the air. She couldn't believe what her eyes were seeing, so she stood up and got closer to the window. She was mesmerized and wanted to touch the droplets of rain, but she was too afraid to open the window.

"Out of nowhere, a lightning pierced the mysterious clouds above the house and went straight toward the windows. Miraculously, the window didn't get hit. The lightning stopped right in front of the window, forcing Sydney to take a few steps back. Gradually, the lightning transformed itself into a gigantic ladder, and a loud friendly bark from outside captivated Sydney so much that she decided to open the window. Then another loud bark was heard from all the way above the clouds and a voice said to her, 'Don't be scared, Sydney. Just step on the ladder and start climbing up.'

"Sydney stepped on the ladder carefully, and as she started ascending the ladder, the raindrops began to vanish in the air one by one in front of her as she touched them. The higher Sydney climbed, the more frightened she became. And every time she thought about going back, another loud bark was heard from above followed by the same words: 'Don't be scared, Sydney. Keep on climbing!'

"So Sydney kept on climbing, and when she finally reached the top of the ladder, up on the clouds, she got the biggest surprise of her life. Bella, her furry sister, was waiting for her. And as soon as they saw each other, Bella jumped into Sydney's arms and started to lick her face.

"'Oh, Bella, I missed you so much!' said Sydney to her furry sister.

"'I missed you too! More than you can imagine!' replied her furry sister.

"Sydney's eyes were already flooded with tears of joy, and she couldn't let go of Bella from her arms. 'Bella, can you please go back home with me?' she asked.

"But Bella looked deep into Sydney's eyes and said to her, 'I can't go back with you, but I brought you here because I don't like to see you scared of lightning and I wanted you to know that the sparks you see in the sky are the signs from me to you that I am well and that I still watch over you. But the most important thing for you to remember is that lightning will be our connection from now on. So when you see lightning, you only need to know that it is me, and everything will be all right.'

"Sydney gave her furry sister one more hug and a kiss on her wet, cold nose and went down the ladder back to her parents, who were still asleep. And whatever happened up in the clouds remained a secret between Sydney and her furry sister, Bella."

As soon as I said, "That's the end," with tears in her eyes, my daughter begged me to keep going with the story. She wanted more satisfaction from the ending, and she needed to know if she would ever see her furry sister again and how and when. But by the time I had finished telling the story, the dark clouds in the sky had floated away, and the rain had become a slight drizzle. So I decided to stop the story with that ending, although I promised her that one day I would absolutely continue the story where she could see her furry sister again.

My wife liked the story as well, but as I was getting ready to stand up, she put her hand on my shoulder. She said to me, "I have a better idea. When you'll be ready to continue the story where Sydney will meet her furry sister again, how about you don't put me to sleep so I can also see and hold my furry daughter again?"

All three of us looked at each other and started smiling.

Six months had already passed since Bella became an angel, and the more that time passed, the more she was missed. Natali started bombarding me with text messages and photos of female pit bull puppies again, and there wasn't a day that passed without my daughter asking me if I found a puppy that I fell in love with yet. They were definitely working together trying to get me to agree to adopt a puppy earlier than we discussed.

I was certainly feeling the pressure from them, and I even tried to keep up with the pictures of the puppies that I received from my wife, but none of them got my attention like the one that I received on the morning of November 9. And that picture wasn't just an ordinary picture.

First, I received a picture of our Bella with "Would Bella approve of this one?" written underneath the photo. That was followed by a Web link and then a picture of an adorable tiny puppy that was sitting outside in a garden, surrounded by some yellowish- and grayish-colored leaves, as well as some small green plants. She had a sad but sweet look in her eyes that instantly melted my heart.

My wife had never before sent me a picture of a puppy accompanied by a picture of Bella, asking if our beloved dog would approve of that puppy. So I called her to find out the reason why she added that comment to that picture. And just as I suspected, she wanted to let me know that she had fallen in love with that puppy. And so did I.

By the time I arrived home that day, it was pretty late; but my wife and daughter were still full of energy, happy, and ready to talk to me about that puppy. Sydney already knew about the puppy since Natali shared the picture with her as soon as she came home from school, so they definitely had plenty of time to prepare a speech and ready to prove to me that this puppy was the one I was waiting for.

However, I had to wake up very early to go to Indiana the next day. And because I needed to get some sleep, the girls had to postpone their pleading until the next day. But even though they knew I needed some rest, they still followed me into the bedroom and put me to sleep by talking to me about all the beautiful memories we had with Bella. Good memories that danced throughout my dreams all night long, but when my alarm rang at 3:30 a.m., it felt like I didn't get any rest at all. So after I got myself ready, I poured a large thermos of hot coffee, and by 4:15 a.m., I was out of the house and on my way to my semitruck.

That morning, the roads had very little traffic, so by the time it was dawn, I was already driving in Indiana when the picture of Bella with "Would Bella approve of this one?" written underneath the photo popped into my mind.

I opened the message from my wife again, and then I realized that I never checked the Web link that followed Bella's picture. So I did. The very first thing that appeared was the puppy's name, and right below was her picture. Right then, something clicked in my mind, and

I remembered the end of my story "The Furry Sister" that I made up for my daughter during the thunderstorm. The part when Bella said, "So when you see lightning, you need to know that it is me, and everything will be all right."

I already knew that the puppy was a female pit bull mix since Natali's only Web-searching criteria was for that breed and nothing else. But when I looked at the puppy's name again, I still couldn't believe what I saw. It simply said, "My name is Lightning."

And as I began to scroll down the page to find out that Lightning was only six weeks old, my heart started to beat faster, and my hands began to shake. That meant Lightning was born just a few days later after my story "The Furry Sister" was born. And I knew that my story would never have been born if Natali wouldn't want to unpredictably ask us all to go upstairs to watch the thunderstorm, and it definitely never would have been born if Sydney didn't agree to watch it as well. The story "The Furry Sister" certainly needed all of us to come alive, and Lightning's birth right after couldn't be just a coincidence.

Cold chills began traveling through my body while my eyes started to flood with tears. I pulled off to the side of the road to find the contact information for Lightning, and as soon as I saw Mending Hearts Animal Rescue, I knew my broken heart would have another chance. I immediately called the contact number, but I had to leave a message, and I also sent an e-mail specifying that I was very interested in adopting Lightning.

Four hours passed after I left messages, and I still didn't hear from anyone regarding Lightning. So I called again and left another message. Another hour passed before I finally received a call back. It was Lightning's foster mom, and she wanted to let me know that she received my messages, as well as my e-mail, but I was the second person in line who contacted her to adopt Lightning.

My heart stopped for a moment. I felt like I was going through the same scenario I went through eleven years ago when I found Bella, but I was ready to fight again. I wasn't going to quit until I would bring Lightning home. So I gathered my courage and decided I would share my story about why I felt Lightning was destined to be in our family.

Lightning's foster mom wanted what was best for the puppy. After she took the time to listen to everything I had to say, she sent me an adoption application online; and gratefully the following day, I received the best e-mail ever. I was approved for Lightning's adoption.

I was overjoyed and couldn't wait to pick her up, but because she was only six weeks old, I'd have to wait until Lightning was eight weeks old and had all her immunization shots. That meant she would be available to be picked up just after Thanksgiving, but I still wanted to keep it as a surprise that I already adopted Lightning.

However, Natali was making it tough for me since she kept talking about how cute Lightning was and how lucky the family would be that would adopt her. And when I saw the sorrow in her eyes when she read on the rescue website that Lightning was no longer available for adoption, I decided to confess to her but still kept it a secret from Sydney.

We both couldn't wait for the day after Thanksgiving to arrive so we could finally go pick up Lightning. But few days before Thanksgiving, as I was reading through my e-mails on my phone, I noticed I had just received a new e-mail from Lightning's foster mom. It said that Lightning would have her last round of shots on Wednesday afternoon the day before Thanksgiving and that Lightning would be available on Thanksgiving. So if we were interested in picking her up on Thanksgiving morning around 10:00 a.m., she would be happy to have Lightning ready for us.

I called her right away, and after I let her know that we would be thrilled to go there on Thanksgiving Day to meet and bring Lightning home, she gave me her address and explained me where to park when we would get there.

It was a two-hour drive from our house, so the night before Thanksgiving, I told my daughter that I had to go someplace to pick up some parts for my semitruck and that I would really love it if we could all go together so I wouldn't have to be alone on Thanksgiving Day. She wasn't too excited knowing that she would be stuck in the car for hours, but she did it for me. By 8:00 a.m. on Thanksgiving Day, the three of us were in the car on our way to pick up Lightning, and we were a little more than halfway there when I was thinking to myself that everything worked out perfectly until I could hear my daughter tell me from the back seat, "Daddy? You know what? You're ruining our Thanksgiving by keeping us in the car. After you pick up the parts for your truck, can we go get a puppy?"

I couldn't believe what I just heard. Sydney definitely believed me when I told her that we were going to pick up some parts for my truck and she couldn't possibly have any clue about where we were really going, especially since we weren't having any pet-related conversation or dropping any hints about what we were really going to pick up. So I tried to avoid answering her question by checking the directions on my phone and shared with everyone that we were only twenty minutes away from the destination.

Sydney's excitement level was still at zero while my wife and I were dizzy with excitement, but we couldn't even show it.

When I looked again at the directions, I realized that we were just a block away from Lightning's foster home, so I slowed down and started to pay close attention to the numbers on each house. We were about four houses away, and we started looking for the parking lot that the foster mom told me to park in since we couldn't park on the street. We passed two more houses, and then we noticed a big building with two crosses on the front door, followed by its parking lot where I was told to park. The building was an old church, and as we drove into its parking lot, I said to my wife, "No way! What are the chances that we are picking up . . . ?" But I immediately shut my mouth and stopped talking when I realized that I almost ruined the surprise for Sydney.

I parked and stepped out of the car, and as soon as we were ready to walk toward the foster house, we heard a woman saying hello to us from the other side of the fence. She opened the side gate that led to the old church parking lot, and after we introduced ourselves, she invited us into her home.

As soon as we walked inside, we spotted a young boy holding Lightning on his lap on the couch while he was watching television. The young boy knew the reason why we were there, so he put the puppy down, and then he left the room. The puppy slowly started to come toward us while two other dogs behind a doggy gate in the kitchen started to bark.

The look of confusion in my daughter's eyes was indescribable. She still didn't have any clue what was really happening. But when I told her that we weren't there for any truck parts and revealed our secret reason for being there, Sydney's eyes lit up like a Christmas tree, and she quickly gave me a huge hug.

When we crouched down to say hello to Lighting, one of the dogs in the kitchen began barking much louder, and she was intensely focused on us. She would not stop barking, and that's when we learned from Lightning's foster mom that the barking dog was Lightning's mother and her name was Sky. We didn't know anything about Sky until then, but after we heard her name and her story, it just reassured me and my wife that Lightning was truly meant to be in our family.

Sky was a dog that was placed into a shelter, and sadly, she was scheduled to be euthanized like so many other shelter dogs. But fortunately, two hours before her time was to come to an end, she was saved and taken into the foster family's home who was working with Mending Hearts Animal Rescue organization. Many foster families couldn't take Sky because they already had a pet in their care, but luckily for Sky and us, this big-hearted family we met decided to foster Sky even though they already had another foster dog.

Even more miraculously, if Sky wouldn't have been saved from the shelter, nobody would have known that she was pregnant with our puppy, Lightning. And what was more interesting was that Sky wasn't rescued from just some random shelter. She was rescued from the Chicago Animal Care and Control shelter, which is the same shelter my wife and I rescued and adopted our beloved dog, Bella.

Once I finished signing the adoption paperwork, my wife took Lightning into her arms, and after we said thank you and goodbye to her mother, Sky, we wished the foster mom a happy Thanksgiving, and then we walked out of the house. And as I was holding my daughter's hand, I looked at my wife holding our Lightning in her arms and couldn't feel more blessed than to have our circle of love completed again on a Thanksgiving Day in the parking lot of an old church.

So I raised my head toward the sky with gratitude and thanked God for the perfect ending to my story— the ending where Sydney could have her furry sister back in her life again and her mommy was not asleep and she could hold her furry daughter in her arms once again.

I hugged them all and said, "Let's go back home."

Bogdan Octavian Sopterean

Bogdan Octavian Sopterean was born on October 1, 1980, in Cluj-Napoca, Romania, which is located in the beautiful region of Transylvania—yes, the region where Dracula was born. When he began middle school, he started to practice martial arts, which helped him to become more focused in school work and helped him learn to believe in himself. At age seventeen, he was already part of the Romanian National Karate Team.

He graduated from Nicolae Balcescu High School, where Spanish, English and Romanian were his major courses. Because sports were already a big part of his life, he graduated from Babes-Bolyai University in Cluj-Napoca, Romania, with a Bachelor's Degree in Physical Education and Sports.

In 2002, Bogdan decided to move to America, known as the land of opportunity, where one could achieve anything they put their mind to, no matter who they are, and ever since, he looked for his calling.

His true passion for writing came at a difficult time in his life, but at that moment, he discovered that writing books is his calling and that he will never stop writing.

Presently, Bogdan and his lovely wife live in Illinois with their sweet nine-year-old daughter and their dog.